SNAPSHOTS

Stories of My Life

by SANDY SOLOMON

First edition

ISBN: 978-1-945493-43-0

Cover art by Terri Behar

This book was professionally typeset on Reedsy.
Find out more at reedsy.com

For my wonderful Paul and our loving family.

Acknowledgement

I could never have finished this without the help of Mark H. Newhouse, author of the award-winning The Devil's Bookkeepers. I also want to thank his son, Keith, for making my dream come true.

SNAPSHOTS: STORIES OF MY LIFE

THE POWER OF WORDS

My husband and I offered to teach English to an immigrant couple from Russia. We discovered that the best way to communicate with them was pantomime. But how do you teach them words like flower and flour? The sound is the same when you enunciate them. English is such an idiomatic language that we purchased a book of idioms to help us. We were glad to have been born in the USA, and not have to learn English as our Russian friends did.

My husband and I once went to a program called Marriage Encounter. Its goal was to help us gain knowledge about each other through writing. We had already been married for over 20 years! How much more could we learn about each other just from writing? At least that is what we thought.

How wrong we were.

The experience began with our being sequestered together in a hotel over a forty-eight-hour weekend without a telephone or TV. We were given a series of questions and allotted a specific amount of time to write our thoughts and feelings about the various subjects. The trick was we had to complete the questions while in separate rooms.

After each segment, we gave our writing to each other to read. What revelations we discovered about each other astonished me. It was like a rocket blasting off into space and discovering new worlds that we thought we knew. We both learned that when you take the time to express yourself by writing, a whole new world of your relationship opens up. We continued to write to each other for many years and it helped.

So, written words, we learned, are a great way to communicate. Within the walls of this book, I hope to share some written snapshots of my life with words and feelings that mean something special to me. I hope you enjoy this journey we are about to venture on together.

SNAPSHOT 1

1935: A NEW YORK GIRL

Announcing
a Recent Arrival

BIRTH ANNOUNCEMENT: Sandra Meiseles (September 12, 1935, 7lbs. 6 oz.)

I'm from cheesecake and strip steaks – a girl from New York City, which is divided into five boroughs. The largest is Brooklyn, where I was born in 1935. It was during Franklin Delano Roosevelt's presidency, after the Great Depression of 1929, caused by the stock market crash. FDR, as he was referred to, had to deal with his own handicap, because he had polio when he was younger. His illness affected his legs, but he was determined to improve the country and placed America's needs above his own. Was he successful? He was the only president to serve four terms in office. His determination and hard work helped end the depression and defeat the Nazis in World War II. Despite his disability, he refused to give up. It was a lesson I learned and endorse.

My parents were concerned about raising another child during this bleak time. They already had a five-year-old son, and along came Sandy, another mouth to feed. Over time, they said that I brought them good luck.

Living with my family, even in hard times, I learned home is the heart of the family and I learned to value traditions. I came to believe a home is more than a place; it is where family members are born, married, and celebrated. It is also where some eventually die and are mourned. With lots of love and determination, you make that home worthy of your family's caring. No matter how hard it can sometimes be, you persevere, and you succeed.

The Depression made things very difficult, but some good events also happened during my early life. The Social Security Act was signed into law and helped people survive the terrible economy. Amelia Earhart caught the world's attention, and the attention of every little girl as the first female to fly solo across the Pacific Ocean. Parker Brothers released a new game,

Monopoly, which is still popular today. Mickey Mouse debuted in a nine-minute animated technicolor film, along with Donald Duck for the first time. That was amazing to see. I still love Mickey and Donald, even if Mr. Duck is a bit crabby.

SNAPSHOT 2

MY CITY

I loved exploring New York City's five boroughs. All are attached by a subway system with bridges and tunnels for cars. One exception was Staten Island where you needed to take a ferry to reach it. That was an enjoyable ride and pretty inexpensive.

New York City was an exciting place to grow up. It is home to the New York Stock Exchange and famous for the Statue of Liberty in New York harbor. Immigrants were thrilled to see the Statue welcoming them to America with her glowing torch. I was thrilled when I first visited Lady Liberty too. Not far was Ellis Island, the processing venue for most immigrants. And, of course, there were St. Patricks Cathedral and Temple Emanuel, massive monuments to New York City's diverse faiths.

Central Park, a favorite place to visit, covers about twenty blocks in the heart of this amazing metropolis. Madison Square Garden is larger than a city block and was where the famous Ringling Brothers Barnum and Bailey circus came every April for a few weeks. Sporting events, as well as all different kinds of entertainment, filled the halls of that arena. What a fun place to visit even way back then.

Radio City Music Hall was another favorite treat. A magnificent showplace, larger than a city block—almost everything in Manhattan was larger than a city block—was where we would see amazing shows. They would start with a live organ concert, followed by an eye-popping show featuring the Rockettes, a precision dance team. And it would all end with a new movie. My parents took us every year for the Easter and Christmas shows, even if they were a little expensive. Those shows were among my happiest childhood memories.

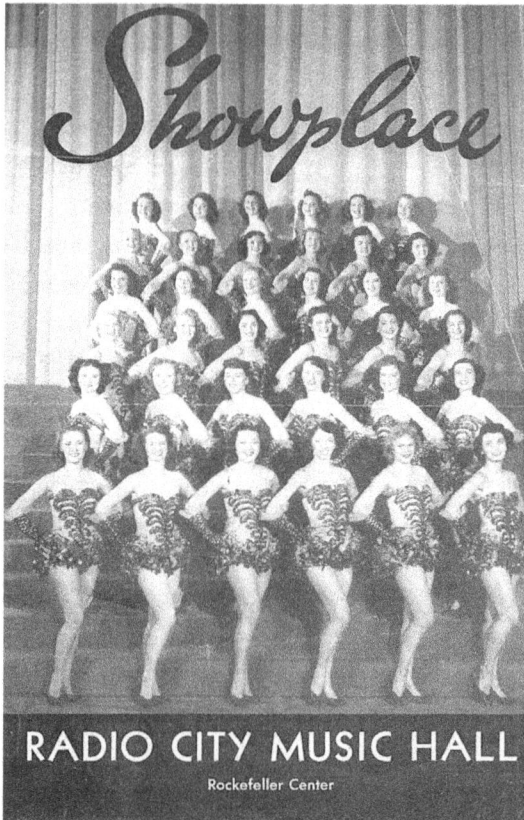

When I was around thirteen, my friends and I formed a club. We called it the Rockettes. We had sweaters made with the club's name on the back. We then went to see a show at Radio City Music Hall. Tony Martin, our favorite singer, was going to be the headliner entertainer. We sat in the front seats in this huge theatre that held thousands of people, waiting for the show to begin. After the Rockettes did their dance routine, Tony Martin came on stage and sang his classic song, "For

Every Man, There's A Woman." We yelled back, "Here we are." He laughed and then continued to sing. We were thrilled he had paid attention to us.

At that time, The Empire State Building, in the heart of the city, was the tallest building in the world. I went there with friends when I was older. I was amazed to go to the top and see the whole city for the first time. What an incredible sight, looking down at buildings looking like small toys.

Living in New York, we were surrounded by museums for the arts and sciences. They were a great way to spend the day without spending a lot of money.

Broadway shows rounded out the opportunities for top entertainment. There were multiple theaters on blocks after block. New York City, in the borough of Manhattan, was, and still is, the entertainment capital of the world.

But there is something else I love about New York.

New York is also known for its pizza. I always tell my friends in Florida there is nothing like a New York Pizza. People always ask, "What is so special?" I won't reveal the secret, but it is the extra oil that is used. We learned that from my grandson, Sean, who was working in a pizzeria. When it closed, he was looking for another job and found an ad on his smartphone looking for a New York pizza maker. He went for the interview and got the job. The only problem: it turned out to be in New Zealand.

Sean was hired, given free roundtrip airfare, and an apartment for three months, as part of the deal. His Dad, Mike, was so shocked, that even though his son was in his 20s and smart enough to make decisions, he remarked, "Are you sure you're not going into slavery?" He stayed in New Zealand for almost a year and then returned after some disappointments to the USA, moving to Florida to join his parents.

SNAPSHOT 3

LIFE IN BROOKLYN

Brooklyn had many sections, and we lived in Brownsville. It was considered by most to be middle class, and life was simple. During that era, a milkman delivered milk to your front door. The iceman carried a tong with a large piece of ice on his shoulder and brought it up to your apartment to keep your food cold in the icebox. This was before refrigeration came into use. Your clothes and linens were taken to a Chinese laundry where they were washed, because there were no electric washers or dryers in most apartments.

It is difficult to imagine, but there were no supermarkets. You purchased your meat from a butcher and it was fresh and cut to your order. Dry goods and canned food, you bought at a grocer, and your produce from a green grocer. (The grocers weren't green, but sold vegetables and fruits.) The local bakery provided the cakes, cookies, and bread. I loved the smells of all those fresh cookies and pies. There was even a store that sold different varieties of cheese, and another that sold pickles and sauerkraut and the like. I remember the pickles were in barrels marked "sour" and "half-sour." You just pulled out the pickle you wanted and it was fresh and crisp. Yum!Yum!

Even to buy a chicken, you went to the fresh market. There they chopped off the head of the chicken, plucked off the feathers, and cut out the gizzards, which were included with the other parts you ordered. The chicken eggs were cooked in the soup with the rest of the chicken. My brother and I competed to eat the delicious eggs.

Everything was fresh and there was no plastic pollution. Was it better? Without refrigerators, and having to go to all these different stores, moms may have had more work, but I loved and still miss all those wonderful smells and tastes that were part of my childhood in Brooklyn.

In those prehistoric days, we had lots of salesmen come to our house. I remember insurance was sold door-to-door. Small sums of money were collected each month by these agents and recorded in a book by hand. My family had to save for the next time the salesman showed up for our next payment. As I said, money was tight, but insurance was important to my father, and so, every day, a small amount was set aside. It was his way of protecting his family, another valuable lesson learned.

Personal service was important way back then. The idea for entrepreneurship grew from savvy individuals seeking ways to make a living by reaching out to the customer, figuring out what they wanted, and making it more convenient. I recall when I gave birth, diapers were made of cloth, the soiled diapers were picked up by a vendor, and clean ones were returned. I know that is hard to imagine today, but people found ways to make a living by being inventive and willing to work hard.

Things change. Years later, my brother and I talked about our favorite meal growing up. It was a special dinner that our mother served on some Sundays. She opened cans of vegetables, set the cans in boiling water, and when they were heated, placed the variety in a circle on our plates, with mashed potatoes in the middle. She then put a poached egg on top of the potatoes. When you broke the yolk, it ran all over the vegetables. My brother said that no one else could understand it, except us. I suppose today a lot of things we thought were special would be difficult to understand.

In my father's youth, apartment houses had only one toilet on each floor. That's right. They had to be shared by the floor's tenants. Toilet paper was not offered. People had to use newspaper instead. Could that be where the term "smart ass" came from?

An indoor private toilet was considered an additional room. You often had to pay extra rent for that luxury. Imagine that today.

I spent my first two years of life in the apartment building of my birth. It was 525 Powell Street, in Brooklyn.

Do you believe in coincidence? A lifetime later, after I retired, we moved to The Villages in Florida. I met a lady from Brooklyn. When I inquired where she lived before coming to The Villages, she replied it was in Brownsville on Powell Street. Curiosity got the best of me, and I asked, "What number?" She responded, "525." It blew me away to hear that. What a coincidence. It amazed me how many people in Florida are former New Yorkers and share my memories of a simpler life.

When I was young, my mother always told me to be a good person. She said, "Your past catches up to you." I think that is one of the most important messages she gave me. It guided me throughout my life. I always tried to be a good person and hope my book passes that message to my future generations.

I'm a Floridian now, but still strip steak and cheesecake. I'll always be a New Yorker and a 'good girl.'

SNAPSHOT 4

1943: EIGHT YEARS OLD

Changes keep happening in life, and I learned you have to change with them. The average wage in 1943 was $2000.00 a year. Hard to believe.

The first major change in my life was when my father was drafted into the Army in 1943, during World War II. With less income to support us, my mother decided we had to move into housing we could afford.

In 1935, the first housing projects were launched in New York City. We could take advantage of paying $25.00 a month for an apartment, so we moved to Williamsburg, another section of Brooklyn.

The city housing project was unique because it was built around cul-de-sacs, and the four-story buildings were attached in a semi-circle. Elevators were not the norm in many four-story buildings back then. If you lived on the upper floors, you could visit a neighbor by going up on the roof, cross over to another building, and go down to their floor by stairs. The roofs were also useful during the hot summers. Families took their bedding from the apartments and slept on the roof to escape the heat. Lying there and looking up at the stars gave you the feeling that you were part of the universe. I loved looking up at the stars on those hot summer nights.

The city housing projects did not make you feel unhappy, nor unworthy. They were for working-class families that had a lower income. We had pride in ourselves and our surroundings.

There was also no need to have a car for transportation. Buses and trains were an integral part of the public transportation system. We went everywhere on them. Plus, we walked a lot, certainly a healthy exercise. I walked to my school—no matter the distance—because there were no school buses. Those came much later.

SNAPSHOT 5

1947: ME AT 12: INDEPENDENCE

Another big change came when I got older. Around 12 years old, my independence became important to me. My friends and I would take a bus or a train and visit the downtown areas of the city, which offered entertainment and shopping. Our parents had no fear that this wasn't a safe activity, as crime and assaults were practically non-existent. Some things do not change for the better. How many parents would send their children on a bus or train alone today?

Accessibility to a nearby bridge allowed us to cross over to another borough, Manhattan. A bus did cross the bridge, but we didn't have much money to spend, so we walked.

Our destination was a recreation center, part of the Jewish Federation called the Educational Alliance, which we called the "Edgies." Another coincidence: I met a fellow recently who had lived in Manhattan during this time, and frequently went to the "Edgies." It was like a magnet.

As young teenagers, we needed our independence. That was our motivation for these excursions. You just did it because you could.

There's an old saying, "You can take the girl out of Brooklyn, but you couldn't take Brooklyn out of the girl. I guess some things do not change.

SNAPSHOT 6

1946: A WORLD AWAY

"Hot Time In The City," and a girl living in Brooklyn, New York. Any way you could get out of the city in the summertime was a treat. My treat came by way of the recreation center of the Jewish Federation. They offered two weeks at a camp in the mountains. You had to apply and wait for them to accept you.

Luckily, I was accepted. I spent time there in July, from 1946 to 1949. It was a break for me, but it was also a break for my parents. They toiled in the city, but now had a little time to just be with each other.

My older brother, Murray, went to a boys' camp at the same time, also from the Federation.

The world underwent another change. World War II was over, and peace was declared. The United Nations was formed with Eleanor Roosevelt, the former First Lady, as the United States delegate. Everyone hoped that with the new world organization, countries would mediate problems, and not cause wars in the future. It was a time of hope and yet sadness over the many lives lost in the war.

But I was still a child and innocent, a world away from the

woes of mankind. It was a time when I was absorbing new vistas and loving them as I loved the colors of a rainbow. In the summer of 1946, I was heading towards an adventure in the mountains, about eighty miles north of New York City, a short distance from the western border of Connecticut. The long two-hour drive didn't deter me from being excited about what awaited me.

A snapshot image of the topography we were passing: it was filled with huge oak trees and various size plants in glorious shades of red and yellow. As new vistas came into view, I felt awakened to a different world, a contrast from the dull gray apartment buildings of the city that we left behind. It was spell-binding and I couldn't stop staring out the window.

Our destination was Camp Solomon. As the bus pulled into a clearing, I could see wood cabins set a distance apart from each other. There was a large main hall, many sports facilities, and a huge lake that looked so inviting to me.

From the ages of ten to twelve years, I witnessed that same view, in total splendor for 2 weeks. I can still see it now.

At Camp Solomon, I participated in many types of sports and crafts. In my last year, twelve years old, I discovered I was a thespian. I could sing and act. Here was a shy girl stepping in front of an audience, revealing herself through becoming a character in a play. I never thought I could do that. As I became braver, my talent allowed me to become the lead. Remember, it was an all-girls camp, so we played the male and female roles. My lead part was as Curly, a cowboy, in Oklahoma, a Broadway show which debuted in 1943.

The
PLAYBILL
for the St. James Theatre
"OKLAHOMA!"

A Musical Play
Based on "Green Grow the Lilacs" by Lynn Riggs
Music by RICHARD RODGERS
Book and Lyrics by OSCAR HAMMERSTEIN 2nd
Production directed by ROUBEN MAMOULIAN
Dances by AGNES de MILLE
Settings by LEMUEL AYERS   Costumes by MILES WHITE
Production Reproduced by JEROME WHYTE
Orchestra Directed by Aaron Benar   Orchestrations by Russell Bennett

(Program Continued on Page 2)

Performing in Oklahoma at Camp Solomon

Amazingly, in only two weeks, we put on this musical show, costumes and all. Learning all the lyrics and dialogue was monumental in that short amount of time, especially for kids who were far from being professionals. But we accomplished it. We rehearsed while still participating in the many other activities the camp offered. The show was a big hit for the campers and the parents who came up to enjoy it. Being a part of that show was a highlight of my last year as a camper.

The irony of my connection to Camp Solomon is that in later years, the love of my life, my husband, was Paul Solomon. Some coincidences are wonderful.

SNAPSHOT 7

1947: MYSTERY SOLVED

Throughout my early years, I used to wonder why I didn't look like either of my parents. They would joke that I was adopted. I believed it was a joke, but I always had that uncertainty in the back of my mind. It sometimes made me feel as if I was in an alternate dimension, unsure of everything.

In the Summer of 1948, when I was about to reach 13 years old, a veil was removed from my mind. A revelation came streaming through with a force that made me realize that I did belong to my family. All doubts were erased.

It happened when I went to visit my father's sister, Aunt Freida, and her family. They lived in Revere Beach, Massachusetts. It was a break from Brooklyn again. I spent a month with the Grossman family. How delightful to spend time within walking distance from the beach and frolic in the ocean. My two younger cousins were fun to be with and we found many ways to entertain ourselves.

My cousins would kid me about my New York accent, and how funny and different it was from a New England one.

I said, "What makes you think I have the accent? It could be your variation."

To which they responded, "Massachusetts was settled first, before New York, so we're right."

I could not argue with that.

Many things that I was used to in New York were different in Massachusetts. A soda was called, 'pop.' Ice cream in a cup—that I called a 'dixie'—to my cousins was a 'hoodsie.' An 'ice cream pop' was a 'chocolate covered' in Revere Beach. A movie theatre was a "cinema" in their world. In New York, theatres were open all day and night, but in Revere Beach, only at designated times. I just went along with the flow and enjoyed the contrasts. When I came home a month later, my parents laughed that I had a New England accent.

One day, I went into their downtown area with my Aunt Freida and her daughters. My aunt met an acquaintance, who thought I was my aunt's daughter. What a surprise and laugh to Aunt Freida, who said "Oh, no." The friend remarked, "Oh, she looks just like you." To me, it was a delightful and warm revelation. I looked like my aunt, and knew I belonged to my family.

SNAPSHOT 8

FAMILY TIES

We don't choose our families, something we are often told. My daughters always wished that we had more family connections, and I used to wish that same thing when I was growing up. Sometimes, that doesn't happen.

MOM'S FAMILY

My mother had five siblings. Two brothers died as youngsters. Her sister, Florence, met a guy at a USO dance after World War II, who hailed from Belgium. She fell in love, married, and moved to Belgium where she gave birth to my cousin, Andrea.

In addition, Mom had another brother who was, unfortunately, mentally unfit. He could not hold down a job, nor take care of himself. He lived with us for a time until he died.

Lastly, she had another brother, Sam, who had his act together. He married and became a father of four daughters. Unfortunately, Mom and Sam did not get along and stopped talking to each other. I liked my Uncle Sam, who as a postman always had stories to tell. Mom said she believed his stories were not true. I never knew why she felt this way. Sadly, I was no longer allowed to see him, his wife, and my cousins. When I got older, I could not find him and always regretted that loss.

DAD'S FAMILY

My father also had five siblings. He had a brother, Charlie, but they stopped talking to each other before I was a teenager, after they argued. Then there were four sisters, three of whom my dad didn't get along with most of the time and he severed those relationships.

Freida was the fourth youngest sister and lived with her family in the suburbs outside Boston. It was her family that I stayed a month with in my early teens. She was delightful to be with when we visited. Her two daughters, who were younger than me, were also pleasant to be around. This was the family connection that made me feel like part of a pod, part of a family that belongs to each other. Sadly, Freida became ill with cancer in her later years. I remember telling my husband that I was going to be by her side before she died. I went to visit with her because I had such warm memories of the few times we had spent together. Freida's daughters married and then divorced, and we lost touch with each other as they moved far away.

MY BROTHER

My brother Murray and I, from when we were young, would talk about family issues. We vowed we would never have an argument. We kept that vow until he died a few years ago at the age of 84. He was five years older than me but always treated me well.

COUSINS

Most of my cousins, who I had known over the years, came in and out of my life because of disagreements between our parents. I was always saddened by the loss of these connections, especially when my friends talked of their Cousins Clubs that got together periodically. That sounded like a lot of fun. I really wanted to have that kind of family.

My cousin, Andrea, Florence's daughter, moved back to the United States when she was 18, after her mother died. She had been brought up in Belgium, but was actually a U.S. Citizen. This is because my aunt returned to Brooklyn to be with her Mom, my grandmother, when she became very ill and then died. Aunt Florence was pregnant at the time and gave birth to Andrea while she was here. That made Andrea a U.S. Citizen.

Andrea's brother was also a citizen because of his mother until he was twenty-five years old. He chose not to continue his citizenship after that.

I became close with Andrea, but she had many troubling issues over the years. She tried going back to Belgium but could not get a job there because she wasn't a citizen, even though she grew up there. She became an alcoholic over time, but through AA she believed she had overcome the addiction.

Andrea was living in New York while I was in Tampa when she called me early one morning. She sounded very distraught. During our conversation, I realized she was drunk. Her last words were that I should remember and tell others that she was a good person. She then hung up.

I was afraid that Andrea was going to kill herself. My husband had not yet left for work, so I relayed the conversation I just had with Andrea to him. We decided to call the police where she lived. When they arrived at her home, she was indeed drunk and despondent. She was angry that I intervened. After that, she stopped talking to me for a long time. Andrea has since suffered a stroke and is homebound.

My husband, Paul, had similar family situations. The brothers on his father's and mother's side showed no interest in keeping in touch, for reasons of which we were never fully aware. Therefore, the cousins had no interest in our side of the family either. The only exception was my mother-in-law's sister, Yetta, who never had children with her husband. She doted on Paul and his sister, Lee, and was a charming person. We visited her many times over the years. One time when we lived in Tampa, she came to stay with us for two weeks. Amazingly, she came with just a duffel bag, but explained that it held a lot of clothes because you rolled them up.

I recall that Yetta always wanted to see a male strip show before her life was over. She suggested I contact my friends and she would take us all to the show. So, we all went. She loved the performances, and we all laughed with her as the guys joked around throughout their routines. Yetta was a character, but we all had a great time.

My daughter, Debra, who lived near Yetta in New York, made sure to visit her years later when she was in a nursing home. Paul was in touch with one cousin, Syd, and together they kept in contact with Aunt Yetta.

I always felt that it was important I reach out to make some contact with our cousins. I had two in particular, first cousins, who we got to see each other at rare times. Even though my father's sister, Molly, did not keep in touch, I did make contact with her son, Murray, on a regular basis. When I was around nine years old, I had a crush on him. While he was in the Navy, I had a photo of him in uniform that meant a lot to me. When I was an adult and married, we made contact again and met on many different occasions. Murray was quite a joker, and lots of fun to be with. He and his second wife, Helen, visited us in Tampa, as well as more recently in The Villages. They were so impressed with The Villages that they considered moving here, but it never happened. He has since passed on, but I'm still in contact with Helen.

My brother, Murray, had three sons. They did not get along with each other. Since Murray died, I've tried to keep in touch with my sister-in-law, and their sons, but that's not working.

In years past, many families were large in number. It makes me sad that so many of us squandered the opportunities to enjoy and learn from each other because of infighting. Was it just jealousy? Or were we more like strangers, unable to make contact as a family?

In our later years, content with our lives, we sometimes share our memories with our siblings. In retrospect, we all recognize that, despite our separations, and distance, we were important to each other and cared that our various branches bore fruit.

SNAPSHOT 9

1949: A BIG MOVE

"School Days, School Days. Dear old golden rule days." A song of yesteryear. I enjoyed school days, the rhythm of learning, and the challenges that came with it. Living in New York City as a student, we had access to many sources of knowledge and stimuli throughout the year. Bus trips took us to multiple museums, the Statue Of Liberty, and zoos, all within easy reach. The city was rich with learning opportunities. By comparison, years later, and in different locales, my children could take only one overnight trip a year.

Apartment living offered us the opportunity to mingle with others of different backgrounds and cultures. Just walking in the hallways, you could smell the various aromas of cooking, and you wished to be invited to eat in that home.

In 1949, as I was about to graduate from Junior High School, we moved to a different part of Brooklyn. With two months left of my senior year, I wanted to graduate with my friends. My teachers thought I should find a way to remain in my classes. Solution found: I would take two buses for almost an hour from my new home to school. I was only fourteen years old, but I was determined to manage it. And thankfully, even though traveling so far might have discouraged some students, I was successful.

Moving to our new locale, I was apprehensive but elated at the same time. I felt like Christopher Columbus, setting out across an ocean and not knowing what was waiting for me. I was sorry to give up long-held friendships, but many of those friends also moved to other areas. City Housing Of New York opened other housing projects, a little more upscale. I would have my own room after sharing a bedroom with my brother for most of my life. Most exciting was the realization that I would be closer to the beaches of Coney Island, famous for its attractions and rides, only a short bus ride away.

I was at a new juncture in my life. I was a stranger in a new high school, coming in as a sophomore where others had been since their freshman year. They had already made friendships. Could I fit in?

Moving was not an easy transition, but new experiences mold us to become who we are. Knowledge and practical wisdom are gained from new experiences and the processes of how we face challenges. My mother often told me that though she never went to high school, she sometimes felt she had more common sense than others she met who were given a higher education. From her, I learned to value the common sense gained from experience.

A lot of events were happening in 1949. The first Emmy Awards were given out in the United States. NATO was established between America and European countries as a mutual defense pact. South Africa began apartheid, the separation, and discrimination, against black people. The Republic Of Ireland gained independence from Great Britain. In America, as a teenager, my world continued to open to greater and brighter horizons. I went through some storms but emerged from the dark clouds into the sunshine.

SNAPSHOT 10

MY BEST FRIEND

SANDRA MEISLES
2978 Avenue W
Senior Arista, Math. Office, Gym Sec.,
Off. Class Treas., Spanish Class Sec.
Sandy, Sandy — as sweet as candy,
Everybody thinks she's dandy.

High School Graduation- 1953

A
s I said, my life took a challenging turn when my address changed to a new home and high school. Walking into Madison High School in September 1949, I was a stranger in this vast complex. I was extremely intimidated. All around me students were happily greeting each other after the summer break. I knew no one. After a few days, the light shone brighter when I met Joan.

The friendship was explosive. It was as though I gained a sister I never had. It felt as if a flower burst through the rocky ground in the garden, reaching toward the sun and bringing new color into its surroundings. She became a part of me, an 'appendage' to my soul, and our lives revolved around each other. We were teenagers, reaching to embrace the world around us and savoring the fun of new experiences. The beginning of dating boys was upon us, and we found dances to go to on weekends at local recreation centers. We loved shopping, or just browsing in the retail shops together. And yes, we faced the challenges that unexpectedly showed up as long as we had each other. We also had a circle of other friends with whom we shared our time, but we were most important to each other.

Joan's father owned a restaurant in Manhattan, just off Broadway, which is famous for its shows. With his connections, we frequented the halls of those great performances. For $2.00, we could sit on the balcony and be mesmerized by lavish productions, eagerly waiting as the curtains went up.

In 1950, it was a time of excitement. It was the beginnings of TV shows such as *I Love Lucy* and the show starring outrageous comedian Milton Berle. We sat staring at the tiny screens with miraculous images in black and white. It was the year disc jockey Alan Fried coined the term Rock & Roll for the music our parents hated. Girls were wearing "poodle skirts" with unique designs. They became famous again when we, in later years, wore them at 50s parties. The Diners Club issued credit cards for the first time. Imagine a time before credit cards made shopping with cash obsolete. The average income had moved up to $3,200.00. And the United States was at war again. This time in Korea.

Except for the Korean War, all seemed right in my world. Though high school had its challenges, I was a good student and was at the top of my classes with above 90 average grades. Joan and I continued our close relationship through "sweet sixteen" parties, graduation, boyfriends, and finally, love and marriage. We each had our daughters. Joan named her daughter after me, which made me feel special. What could go wrong?

SNAPSHOT 11

THE UNTHINKABLE

It all collapsed when my daughter, Debra, was about one year old. I was selling Avon Products. Joan's husband, Arthur, called to tell me that he wanted to buy a gift for Joan among the canisters in the Avon collection. I welcomed him into my home the next day.

I was soon shocked he was not there to make a purchase. His intent was sexual assault. My screams and effort to fight him off made him finally give up, and he left.

I could not believe what happened. I thought this only occurred in stories that I read in books. This could not have happened to me. The innocence of my existence was suddenly ripped away. I fled, crying hysterically to my neighbor next door. She was my age with her own little boy. Mickey eventually calmed me down, but with a warning not to tell my husband, Paul, of this incident.

"How can I not tell him?" I exclaimed. "We have a lot of social contact with Joan and Arthur. She is my best friend."

When Paul came home that night, knowing that Arthur was coming, he asked about the visit.

I could not help it. I could not stop the tears that were flowing from my eyes and covering my cheeks. With despair inside me, I related the episode to him. Of course, he became enraged and said he would want to kill Arthur if he ever saw him again. Now the dilemma: what do I do about Joan?

Paul gave me three choices. The first was to tell Joan what her husband tried to do. My response was, "How can I destroy a marriage, even if Arthur was a bastard?"

The second choice was to see Joan only on my own. With even more uncertainty, I said, "How do I handle that when we shared so many times together?"

The third option was the most difficult: end the friendship.

I was in total shock. How could Arthur have chosen me and destroyed a special friendship? The hatred I felt was as though a demon I didn't know existed had risen from inside my body and taken over my mind. How do I cut off an appendage, a part of me? Joan was so near and dear to me. The love that I felt for her sometimes made me wonder if I was a lesbian because it was so strong.

I hated it but felt I had no option but to choose the third choice. I stopped calling Joan and didn't answer the phone when she called. Joan sent me notes. I did not respond. The hardest part for me was that I realized she was the only one who did not understand, who did not know what happened. She must have been so hurt. But what else could I do?

During this time, I found myself crying at the oddest moments. I ended up going into therapy. I needed help trying to work through it. From another friend in the neighborhood, I learned that Arthur was fooling around with another woman. I guessed it was time to tell Joan how despicable he was, but I didn't have the courage. I never shared my secret with her. I could not hurt her again.

I never found a friendship as close again.

SNAPSHOT 12

1952: A HANDSOME GUY

It was the year 1952, a year that began to shape my life. Was it analogous to the start of the reign of Queen Elizabeth II of England, or Dwight Eisenhower, our new President, both beginning their transitions at the time? My life was perhaps on a different scale of importance, but primary to me. It was a time when I began to blossom. I was a flower reaching for the sun, extending leaves, and developing buds that burst open to reveal a beautiful girl eager to find new possibilities. I was shy in one-on-one conversations but could hide that reticence behind words on paper. I had the gumption at age sixteen to write to a complete stranger in the Marines.

At a sweet sixteen party for a friend, I noticed a fellow talking about his buddies in the Marines and showing their photos to a few others. One of the photos of a very handsome guy caught my attention. I asked Marvin if he could give me the Marine's address.

Paul's Pen Pal Photo

Bewildered, Marvin asked why.

I replied, "I thought he might be lonely, far away from home."

I sent my Marine, Paul, my first letter and a photo.

My Photo to Paul- Age 16

Before Paul responded, he contacted Marvin and asked, "Who is this?" Marvin responded, "She's a nice girl."

After a few more letters between us, a pen pal relationship began. Two months later, Paul came home on a furlough. We had our first date. It was a double date with Marvin and his girlfriend.

On our second date, Paul picked me up in a beautiful pink Mercury sedan, courtesy of his father. Was I impressed? I felt like Snow White meeting her Prince Charming. Previous dates with other guys had been traveling on a bus or a train. Upon meeting my parents, Paul had such warmth, and a gift of gab, that I was impressed. It was as though he knew my parents before this first meeting.

Paul took me to a nightclub, and the evening was magical, as we made the connection to each other. Paul told me many years later that on that second date, he knew he was going to marry me.

After one more date, Paul went to California for the remainder of his two-year tour. His first letter back to me started with the salutation, "Darling." But I was still a young teenager not ready for romance. My letters continued to begin with, "Dear pen pal."

SNAPSHOT 13

1953: PAUL OR STAN?

A t the same time I was writing Paul as a pen pal, I was also writing to another guy, Stan, in the Air Force. He had been a friend before he was inducted. Over the years, I had to make copies of the correspondence, so that I wouldn't make a mistake and confuse the two.

During our correspondence for the next sixteen months, Paul's beautiful and warm letters made me realize that he was the love of my life. How do you decide if someone is right for you? How do you find that one human who is meant for you? How do you know if he is the correct match, if your life goals mesh to ensure wholeness? I could feel it at the end of each page that I read over the months Paul and I shared our thoughts on paper. I knew he was the one.

Now I had to write a "Dear John letter" to Stan and let him know that I'd fallen in love with someone else and I would no longer keep up our communication with each other. I felt bad, but I had never indicated anything more than I was his friend keeping in touch. He was in a war zone in Korea, and I believed the correspondence was just my way to cheer him up during that difficult time.

During the sixteen months Paul was in California, he made sure that I got to know his family, and we connected on different occasions. The first time, his father showed up at our apartment to bring me perfume Paul bought in Mexico. His father and mother had gone to California to visit Paul.

The next time I saw them, Paul's parents took me out for my birthday in September, only a few months later. On Thanksgiving, my parents and I were invited to their home for dinner. I remember Paul calling from California to say hello, and his mother getting all excited that a phone call was coming from such a distance, just to say hello to me.

Paul sent me souvenirs of the places he visited on the West coast, and his sense of humor often came through. One day I was contacted by the post office, telling me that there was a large package waiting. I retrieved this very big box and brought it home. Opening it, I kept pulling out paper, and paper, and more paper. At the bottom of the box was a rock with a note, "I didn't know what else to send you from the Rocky Mountains."

My greatest joy came when Paul was discharged in October 1953. We became engaged, and my life became a fairy tale of happiness.

We both kept the letters that we wrote to each other all those years. Twenty-two years later, we had the occasion to take them out of the attic and began to read them to each other. What a 'high' that was. I put those first letters in a frame that is on a wall in my home. It is a wonderful memory of our beginning.

SNAPSHOT 14

1954: LOVE AT NINETEEN

I was about to turn nineteen and I am getting married. My life turned into a whirlwind of activities and plans for a new venture. I am going from having a bedroom of my own to sharing a bed with a man, the touch of another human being, flesh to flesh. No need for a blanket, he will keep me warm and share my dreams. I'm undertaking an experience that had been only a figment of imagination before. It was taking form like a sculpture, becoming a reality. I would be taking another name, another label, a new address. The excitement was overwhelming, but I latched on as if to an ocean wave and rode with it all the way.

In 1954, other changes were happening that made an impact on all our lives. The Women's Right To Vote became a reality after so many years of waiting and struggle. Racial segregation in schools was ruled unconstitutional by the Supreme Court. Both of these major changes made a great difference for Americans and added to my sense of optimism and excitement.

My big day came on October 10, 1954. What a celebration! I should say that Paul wanted me for his birthday present the night before, but my father was not having it. In those days,

41

most of us had to wait until after the knot was tied.

Paul's and my parents went all out with an abundance of food and music for the wedding. I borrowed a beautiful gown and felt as if I had ascended into the realm of royalty as the evening became all about me, something I had never known before. What a feeling I had as the smile never left my face.

At the same time, while I'm on cloud nine, as guests are congratulating Paul before the ceremony, his concern is, "How am I going to take care of another person for the rest of my life?"

When the ceremony was ending, and my handsome husband lifted my veil to kiss me, I wanted to cement those lips to mine forever. He was mine for the rest of my life.

The song that we chose for our opening dance was "Our Love Is Here To Stay," recorded by Nat King Cole. Whenever we heard it during the rest of our lives together, it was always special.

"It's very clear, our love is here to stay
Not for a year, but forever and a day…
In time, the Rockies may tumble, Gibraltar may crumble
They're only made of clay
But our love is here to stay."

Many years later, at our 50th-anniversary celebration, we requested that song. The singer never heard of it. We found the original recording, so we could dance again to our favorite song. How could we have known fifty years ago, our love would endure? It truly was a love affair.

Our honeymoon was in Miami Beach, another world for me, who though I had visited Massachusetts, was a New York City girl. I also had never flown on an airplane before. How was my body going to handle flight? I was nervous.

As I was looking out the window, I asked Paul, "What are those lights?"

Paul says, "Sandy, that's the interstate. We're already high up in the air."

I did not even feel the plane take off.

All those firsts for a new bride. Florida was a glorious place to be. We took advantage of all it had to offer as we melded ourselves into our new life with each other.

Our parents could not believe that we chose Florida for our honeymoon. "Who goes to Florida in October, during hurricane season?"

We went anyway and ironically, a hurricane did form while we were there. It was coming from Cuba toward Florida. However, it bypassed Florida, traveled up the Eastern coast, and hit New York City.

SNAPSHOT 15

THE HONEYMOON IS OVER

With my honeymoon over, reality set in, and adjusting to a new role as a wife took precedence over everything else. I had been in my second year of college, but it became necessary to search for a job instead. Paul went back to school, a technical program. His goal was to work in the up-and-coming computer world. Though the GI Bill paid for his classes, I had to work to pay for our living expenses.

Luckily, in high school, after completing the requirements, I was allowed to take electives in my senior year. I chose typing and stenography, thinking it would be helpful during lectures and correspondence in college. My objective, therefore, was to find a job as a secretary.

What is an employer looking for?

Experience!

Having none, I had to invent it. It was not in my personality to lie, but unfortunately, it was the only way to accomplish my goal. I gave the names of relatives who were in business as my references.

One of my interviews was with a shirt company. They were

located a few blocks away from my parents' handbag business, in mid-Manhattan. When I completed the interview, which I believed went well, I walked to my Mom and Dad's company. Mom handled the front office while Dad was in charge of the workers. When I arrived, Mom was in the back with Dad, so I sat down at her desk. The phone rang, and I answered, "Rosart Handbags."

The caller was given the telephone number as a reference, for me.

My response was, "She was a highly efficient secretary, but it became necessary for us to downsize, so we had to let her go."

After giving myself the best recommendation I could manage, I got a call the next day. They offered me the job.

For the next few years, I worked with the best people and was especially impressed with my new boss, Mr. Gropper, who treated me very well. I stayed a little over two years until I was about to give birth to my first child. In my last months, Mr. Gropper would let me come in late and leave early so that I would miss the heavy load of people on the trains.

Many years later, when we lived in Poughkeepsie, I met Mr. Gropper's son. He recognized me and told me how much his father liked me as his private secretary. I felt good about that, because I felt the same way about his Dad. That experience of working as a secretary always brings a smile to my face as part of the wonderful memories in my life.

So many new events were cropping up in that year, 1955. After many years of children suffering from polio, a crippling disease in the limbs or lungs, the Salk Polio Vaccine was introduced. At the same time, Russia launched Sputnik, the first satellite. It began the space age and a race between the Soviet Union and the United States that took the Cold War into space. Many people were afraid that if the Soviets controlled space, we would be in great danger of attack.

SNAPSHOT 16

NEWLY WEDS AND RICE KRISPIES

As a newly married young couple, we rented a two-room apartment, around the corner from my in-laws. For breakfast, I took out Rice Krispies, a banana, and milk. When Paul first saw my breakfast, he asked, "What's that for?" The only way he ever had Rice Krispies was in chicken soup.

Laughing, I showed him a photo on the box, depicting the three elves, Snap, Crackle, and Pop, sliding down a ramp into a bowl of milk. Paul was bewildered and followed his routine for the rest of our married life. Over 50 years later, we had friends as house guests, and I made chicken soup with dinner. Paul went to get his Rice Krispies. My friend, Barbara, was stunned. She said she had finally found a match to her routine which she had followed since childhood. I did not believe it.

We soon learned that being in close proximity to Paul's parents was not the best situation. Having a key to our apartment, my mother-in-law would come in and clean while I was at work. I felt as if it was an invasion of my role as a wife, and my independence in our marriage. Paul had to explain to her, diplomatically, that I wanted to take care of my own apartment.

One day, Paul's mother stood in front of our second-floor apartment, which faced the front of the building, and called Paul. He opened the bathroom window and shouted down, "What do you want Mom? We're taking a shower." Embarrassed, with people sitting in chairs outside, Mom never showed up unannounced at our apartment again.

My mother was a good cook but made the same meals week after week. I guess that is why I didn't show an interest in learning how to cook from her. Not knowing how to cook had limitations. To add interest, Paul didn't know how to eat. He had his limitations too. He just ate meat and potatoes.

I started collecting recipes, which sometimes sounded better on paper than they turned out. Paul was patient and often reached for his peanut butter and jelly. One time, I even got up the nerve to invite our friends, Syd and Florence, over for dinner. The meal didn't work out as I expected, but my friends understood, as they were newlyweds themselves. Florence invited us the next time for dinner at their home. She made spaghetti and ketchup. I guess we were about even.

Paul and I had a lot of joy and laughter learning and getting used to each other. My Dad once told me, "It's always good to start from the bottom. That's how you appreciate what you've gained as you achieve more in years to come." It worked well with cooking and with the growth of our income as well. After a lot of funny missteps and failed recipes, we found foods I could cook and that would please our palates.

SNAPSHOT 17

1957: IBM AND MOTHERHOOD

Life was different for both of us when Paul was hired by IBM in 1956, after interviews with three companies proved successful. Westinghouse and General Electric, major companies, offered him higher salaries, but Paul believed that IBM was the company on the move for the future. So, it was with the "wisdom of Solomon," relating back to Biblical times, that Paul Solomon made the right choice, and grew with IBM for 35 years.

Adjusting to motherhood was a task. In 1957, when my first daughter was born, there were no courses on how to be a mother at the time, at least none that I knew of. Debra was a "projectile vomiter," which meant that at each feeding, she regurgitated whatever she ingested. Convinced that she was starving, I went to visit the doctor.

After an examination, he said that she had gained weight since birth. That surprised me. Still worried, I asked, "Doc, what is the problem?"

The doctor answered, "I think the problem is the mother."

Actually, the problem was that Debra's stomach valve had not completely closed as of yet but would in time. "Calm down, mother," he said. Looking back on it now, that was good advice. Debra did outgrow that problem.

I lived within walking distance to the grocery store, which I had gone to many times over the years before I became a mother. One day, I placed my daughter in her carriage and walked happily along the avenues to that destination. Debra was asleep, so I left her outside the store to do my shopping. In those years, you felt safe that no one would steal from you. I completed my shopping, and carrying my grocery bags, walked back home. I put my groceries away, and almost fell over. "Oh My God! I left my baby at the store."

Practically running back, I found Debra still sleeping, unaware that her foolish mother had forgotten her. These days, I would have been arrested for neglect. Believe me, I never did that again.

Though babies are the cutest company to have around, I felt the need to do something more. I amazed myself when I got up the nerve to ask my husband to watch our six-month-old baby when he came home from work. I said I would give him dinner first so that I could go door-to-door selling Avon. I was surprised when he agreed.

Avon salespeople had to visit strangers' homes to sell their products. I was still pretty shy. That first knock on a stranger's door, starting up a conversation, and promoting a product was the catalyst that helped me flourish. Selling Avon made me come out of my shell and gain confidence in myself.

It took some time, but Paul said that finding something else to occupy my time had been a good idea. Having our new baby was exciting, but in that world where I would only be with my child, I only would be relating what Debra did. Going out and selling Avon, I brought back into the conversations many different stories. Debra was wonderful but I could not limit myself to four walls and a world without people, conversations, and stories.

In 1964, another World's Fair took place in New York City at Flushing Meadow Park, near Laguardia Airport. It was very exciting for our young family.

We were living in Brooklyn, not far, so we were able to attend the Fair with our three- and seven-year-old daughters.

There was a lot to see with all the exhibits as we traversed the huge grounds. Hertz, the car rental company, built a stroller in the shape of a car that a child could sit in. We pushed our younger daughter around in it.

After a long while, I found that I was getting tired. On a whim, I got into the Hertz replica with my daughters now pushing me. It was quite comical.

A tour train was passing with the guide explaining to the visitors what was going on at the fair. When he saw me, he stopped the train and everyone was laughing, including me.

Mommy being pushed by her children is a sight that was not planned by the officials at the World's Fair. But it is a special memory for me. I knew someday, I would see the world.

SNAPSHOT 18

1958: MOVING UP

"The times they are a changing." In 1958, the U.S. Space Agency (NASA) was established. PAN AM made its first transatlantic flight. Pizza Hut was founded, and microchips, a major part of our computer industry, were introduced.

We were changing as well, moving up to a four-room, two-bedroom apartment in a new neighborhood. It was in a fourteen-story building, where sound traveled throughout this concrete structure.

One humorous situation comes to mind. In the apartment above us lived a family of three. The parents were arguing with their young son, who angrily stormed into his bedroom, which was just above ours. As we lay in our bed, we heard the boy call out, "Good Night." No answer. Again he yelled, "Good Night." No answer. He then shouted, "Isn't anyone going to answer?" My husband finally yelled back, "Good Night."

The building was a few miles away from Idlewild Airport (which later became Kennedy Airport). This close proximity led to flights flying pretty low over our building. A neighbor on the top floor remarked once, "I wondered if I was going to have one hundred people for dinner," because she could almost see their faces in the plane windows.

Other than the noisy planes, the area was delightful. There were playgrounds for the children and lots of spaces for walking. We enjoyed our neighbors, who in this new upscale city housing project, were in the same financial situation as we were.

It was seven years later, a few years after our second child, Judy, was born, that I broached the idea of moving again. Paul's income had increased, so I said, "We need a larger space." Paul believed I meant a bigger apartment.

"No, I think we should buy a house."

"What!" That was his reaction. He was totally in shock. "Are you kidding?"

"I think we can do it. A house is equity that we can build on, instead of paying rent," I said. Paul had to agree.

We started looking on Long Island, adjacent to New York City. 'The Island' was where many young families in Brooklyn headed to when they wanted to buy an affordable house. But due to what we could afford, the housing was far away from Manhattan, where Paul worked. He estimated that commuting on the train, the only means of public transportation, would take two hours each way. It looked as if my dream of owning a house was dead.

SNAPSHOT 19

OUR DAUGHTERS

Though our dream of a new house was on hold, we had another dream fulfilled, the birth of our daughters.

Our daughters enriched Paul and my life together. They brought purpose into our marriage as we sought to help them develop and blossom.

Debra was born on March 17, 1957, and because it was St. Patrick's Day, I went crazy every year with "green" birthday parties. The dress, cake, and decorations all had to be green. I finally let go of that fantasy when she was about 5 or 6 years old, but it was fun while it lasted.

Debra was a happy child and greeted everyone with a smile. As the years went by, she acquiesced to whatever we asked of her. As her parents, we felt pride and satisfaction, as if we made a successful and beautiful creation.

A few years after Debra was born, we decided to have another child. But after an easy pregnancy with Debra, I suffered two miscarriages. The doctors tested both of us. The tests revealed no problems; no answers, so we tried again.

Four and a half years later, on August 3, 1961, out came another beautiful girl, who we named Judy. She was not an easy child to deal with. Interestingly, we heard from others later that a second child is more of a challenge. Judy was tough. She did not welcome others into her world that easily. When she stood in her playpen and someone tried to say hello, she reached out and hit them.

When Judy was a toddler, a friend of mine was helping me one day. She took Judy with her to a store. In the same aisle, another mother was angry with her little boy who was misbehaving. Judy jumped in to admonish the boy. My friend was embarrassed, but laughing inwardly, said "She's not my child."

As Judy grew older, she began to mellow and became a sweet child with whom to share our lives.

We loved our girls, and our family was complete. I totally enjoyed motherhood, and our world was bright as each new day dawned. Everything seemed to go smoothly, until our daughters reached their teen years. Each of them had challenges that were difficult to overcome. Whatever the problem or the pain they were dealing with, I always welcomed them reaching out to me. I was there for them with my love if they let me in. I was there to just wrap my arms around them and give them comfort and peace. My family was so important to me. We were like a tree, and each branch made the tree whole. But as they became young adults, they met those challenges head-on, persevered, and succeeded on their own.

Debra became a nurse. She dealt with her patients beautifully, with warmth and understanding of their delicate situations, which I witnessed one time.

Debra, who was working for Hospice later, was honored as the best nurse in Ulster County, New York State. Families of patients she had taken care of were there, but Paul and I were going on a trip the next day. As we lived in Florida, we couldn't make it to be with her for this special celebration. But we were so proud of her for being so caring and receiving this honor.

Judy always excelled in Math. With that expertise, she found her way into the financial world. She worked for H & R Block, doing well completing taxes for clients. She also worked for a mutual fund company.

As it turned out, both my daughters would play an important role in my later life.

SNAPSHOT 20

IT'S ALIVE

I thought our dream of owning a house was dead. Then we heard a local radio DJ advertise a new development in Central New Jersey, called Yorktowne. He claimed that the time travel into Manhattan, by bus, would be fifty-six minutes (probably in the middle of the night). Intrigued, we decided to check it out.

The community appeared to be in the middle of nowhere, but we were mesmerized by what it had to offer. It was as though we were being offered candy on a stick, the sweetness melting in my mouth, as we learned more and more about buying a house in Yorktowne. You were not just buying a house with all the appliances included. You were buying a new lifestyle, a concept that decades later was the slogan we heard when we retired to The Villages. An enticing recreation club was a unique part of the package, complete with swimming pools and a clubhouse. It promised to be a wonderful change for our little family.

Before we made our decision and signed the papers, we discovered that there was going to be a benefit at Madison Square Garden, a huge arena in Manhattan, with singer Tony

Bennett. But that alone wasn't the main reason for our interest. There was going to be a door prize of the model house we wanted to buy in Yorktowne. Who ever heard of giving a house away as a door prize? You know that we went to the benefit to win the prize.

Oh well, we didn't win. But the event was enjoyable and we went back to Yorktowne. We bought a house.

Our parents were in shock and did not believe that we were leaving the state of New York. They said they would never see us again. But we knew that instead of the long trip by ferry from Brooklyn to Staten Island, and then crossing into central New Jersey, a shortcut was in the works. The Verrazano Bridge was being built and would shorten the trip dramatically. And that is what happened, and our parents were visiting monthly.

My in-laws had the bad habit of visiting us unannounced when we lived in Brooklyn. They tried it once in our new home, showing up without calling in advance. Were they surprised when we weren't home. And they didn't know how to reach us. It was before cell phones were invented. We didn't give them a key, so they had to go all the way back home without seeing us. They never did that again.

Ironically, many years later, when they retired, my parents moved to Florida. How is that for putting distance between us? We understood. One does what fits the moment in our lives. Distance did not change how we felt about each other.

SNAPSHOT 21

PARTIES EXTRAORDINAIRE

For a few years while we lived in Brooklyn, we developed a friendship with two sisters and their husbands, extremely creative individuals. They created the most unusual New Year's Eve parties. The first time we were invited, it was a hillbilly party. It began with an invitation in hillbilly-style prose that specified that we dress as hillbillies.

Upon arriving at their duplex, we saw that the first floor of the house was set up to look like a barn. All the furniture had been removed from the room. We sat on tires. There were rafters on the ceiling and hay was spread across the floor. Our host sat on a ladder. We were given a booklet which contained songs and commentary that we were to follow. Actually, all of the text was humorous, and we laughed and laughed as we read along. There was no need for liquor to make it enjoyable. It was just pure fun. And, of course, there was plenty of food to eat.

The next year, the party was on the upper floor. Once again, furniture was removed from the room. This time, it was a gypsy party, and we had to dress accordingly. The room was set up as a gypsy camp with stars on the ceiling, leaves on the floor, and a covered wagon in the center. Just like before, it was all humor that we enjoyed as we read and sang along with our hosts.

In the third year, our friends moved out of Brooklyn to reside on Long Island. Even though it was far, we went to their party. It was a 'turn-about' theme. All the men dressed as women, and the ladies dressed as men. When the stroke of midnight approached, we lay on the floor in a semi-circle, alternating men and women, our heads on each other's bellies. At midnight, we pulled on a popper, and the sound started us laughing as our bellies went up and down from the humor.

These two couples were so imaginative. We never had so much fun at a New Year's party. However, the following year, we moved away to our new home in New Jersey. I thought I could recreate those creative parties, but I didn't have the imagination, nor the talent. I learned that sometimes you have to accept your limitations and admire those who are so creative and talented.

SNAPSHOT 22

1965: IN THE BOONIES

I t is 1965. The average income is $6,450.00, and the price of gas is 31 cents a gallon. Fashions have changed as women's skirts get shorter and men's hair grows longer. The mini skirt makes its appearance. The entire Northeast region, including New England, becomes embroiled in a blackout that lasts 13 ½ hours. People are stuck in elevators. Life comes to a halt. Many women give birth 9 months later.

The strength of our bonds was about to be put to the test.

We were leaving New York State to branch out into a new realm. We were entering uncharted territory, uncertain whether we could financially manage a new home. Our lawyer told us that we cannot afford the house we are buying, which is $20,000.00. (Seems incredible now.) He told us it was necessary to put down a $2,000.00 down payment to lower the mortgage. As a Marine veteran, Paul was told he did not need to place a deposit on a VA mortgage. But we ended up borrowing the money from my in-laws.

Our new home was in Central New Jersey, in remote Manalapan, which we refer to as Englishtown because that is the most established town in this rural area. And that's not saying too much.

The nearest major shopping area was eight miles away in Freehold. It was in Monmouth County, deeply involved in the Revolutionary War. The area included the Molly Pitcher Inn, where American generals congregated to discuss war tactics. After living in Brooklyn, where everything was easily accessible, this was quite a departure for us.

Before building began, the builders poured wine into the foundation. That was the ceremony that was used in Iraq where they come from. We made sure to be there for the ceremony, so we would have good luck with our new house.

Our home had nine rooms in a two-story dwelling on a half-acre of land. The purchase price included all the appliances in the unusual color of turquoise, which we chose. With all new furniture, we decorated the living room, dining room, and kitchen in shades of turquoise, orange, and black, with white cabinets in the kitchen to set it all off.

We had three bedrooms upstairs, three rooms downstairs for recreation, and a den. It was all very exciting as we sat on our porch and looked out among the few houses that were built already. It was very quiet at night, not anything like the sounds of the city. We could look up into the sky and wonder where all those stars came from. We were mesmerized by the wonders of our new domain, as suburbanites. Our children, now four and eight years old, could walk out into the streets barefooted to play with their friends, since there is hardly any traffic.

Paul bought a used car to take him to the bus stop where he will embark on his trips to work, going along the New Jersey Turnpike and through the Lincoln Tunnel into Manhattan. The fifty-six-minute travel time that was advertised, in reality, takes one and a half to two hours, depending on traffic. Paul sometimes sits next to the Mayor, who is also a commuter. They became friends.

We ascertained that most of our neighbors come from Northern New Jersey or New York City. They must have been listening to the same DJ on the radio as we did.

SNAPSHOT 23

1970: OUR CALLING

O ur next-door neighbor went to the same high school in Brooklyn as Paul did. Our new world in the suburbs was connected by all of our roots to the old. We were surrounded by young couples like us. The family across the street had a five-year-old boy, Joey, who attached himself to Paul, always wanting to help him out. Joey said his daddy doesn't let him help. It was a cute relationship.

One day, I went to the bus stop to greet my cousin, Andrea, who was visiting for a few days. When we got back home, Andrea got out of the car, before I drove it into the garage, and went to meet Paul who is cutting the front lawn on his riding mower. She kisses him hello and walks back into the house. Joey witnessed this and came across the street to talk to Paul who stopped the mower again. "Who's that?" Joey asked.

Paul responded, "That's my girlfriend." He continued on his mower and Joey waited for him to come around. He then said, "What'd you do with the other one?"

Making a lot of new friends was a joy for us and our daughters. We were relishing our community and acclimating well. Our minds and hearts were open to new ideas. The biggest surprise was that we founded a new Temple.

In Brooklyn, we were surrounded by a large number of Jewish people, and I guess that is why my family never officially joined a synagogue. Here in Yorktowne, Jews were a minority in our mixed community. We decided to send our daughter, Debra, to the nearest synagogue, but she hated it and refused to return to her classes. It was an Orthodox ritual, which means it strictly obeyed all Jewish laws and rituals. Even we were unfamiliar and uncomfortable with this form of Judaism.

Talking to other Jewish couples in our area, many who felt the same way, we decided to research a more modern alternative. Before we knew it, eight couples and us established a brand-new Temple, with the help of a Reform organization in New York City. It so consumed us that it was one of the most exciting things we had ever done in our lives, with the exception of becoming new parents and homeowners. Over the years, the congregation grew, renting rooms to hold our meetings in schools and churches. Then, in, 1970, our Temple building was completed. I used to carry a photo in my wallet of the building, the same as a new parent carries a photograph of their child. I felt as if I had given birth again. The first night our temple opened was my daughter Debra's Bat Mitzvah, when she turned 13 years old. A huge turnout certainly made her more nervous, but she did wonderfully, and we enjoyed the whole evening. We provided the refreshments. It was like a wedding reception as we celebrated this joyous occasion. When I was asked, "Who is the caterer?" I responded, "My Mother."

Of course, Paul and I, as well as our daughters, were very active participants in our temple. In the beginning, before we had a building, Paul was the Vice President and I was the Secretary. A business phone for the temple was placed in our home's lower level. As time went by and no calls came in, I waited in anticipation. One day, the Temple phone rang, and I was so excited, I ran downstairs to answer it. The caller said, "This is God. Any messages?" I laughed and laughed. It was my crazy husband.

SNAPSHOT 24

THE BEST OF BOTH WORLDS

A s we were within driving distance to New York City, many times we went into Manhattan to see Broadway shows and celebrate other special occasions. Sometimes for their birthdays, our daughters would ask to see a show on Broadway. IBM always had a big party for Christmas, where they would give out toys for the children of their employees. Usually, that would bring us back to the city.

Madison Square Garden was a big draw. We were living in the best of both worlds, the quiet of suburbia and the excitement of the city.

Over the years, many new communities opened up and the entire area became a big draw for development. The New Jersey Turnpike Authority even talked about extending the turnpike to the edges of Yorktowne. People were in an uproar. Many meetings were held to fight against this change. Our development was in the proposed path, but not our block. I remember one fellow whose property was on the plans, standing and asking, "Just tell me if I should fertilize my lawn." He, and most of us, felt strongly that the Turnpike would threaten our quiet corner of the planet. After many discussions, we were glad the extension was canceled.

We loved that there were still rural areas around us. Debra asked one day if she could go home with a friend in school, and if I could then pick her up. When it was time, I explicitly followed the directions to her friend's house but got lost. There were a few homes scattered here and there. Thinking I should go back to where I started, I tried to make a U-turn. I quickly discovered that you don't make a U-turn on a two-lane country road. I landed in a depression off the surface, with the front of my car facing up. I crawled out of my car and tried to knock on some doors of houses nearby, but it was futile. Standing on the road, hoping to flag down a car, I thought about how I told my daughters not to get into a stranger's car. But what could I do? I didn't have the phone number of Debra's friend's house. A car came along after a while and luckily, he knew the neighborhood. He went up and down the block until he found the house where I was supposed to go.

in New York State, where Paul was transferred to for his work. I recall my friend, Helen, being upset that we were leaving and thinking she would never see us again. I told her that I would always be in touch because when you're my friend, you're my friend forever.

Our friends, Joyce and Jerry, we'd known since our Brooklyn days, and we lived near them in New Jersey also. Over time, they moved to Chicago, and we lost touch with them. Living in Tampa over twenty years later, we were at a party for our friends' 40th anniversary. Some of their friends were from Chicago. I sat at a table with these out-of-towners and listened to them talking about their friends Joyce and Jerry in Chicago. Now Chicago is a very big city, but in my mind, I wondered if it was the same Joyce and Jerry that we had known. Would you believe it was the same couple? How small a world is that? You know we made contact once again with Joyce and Jerry.

Many years later, while touring the upper United States, we made sure to tour Chicago, and visited with Joyce. Jerry died a few years before, but it was such a delight to be with Joyce and just reminisce of the happy times we shared together.

True friends are like glue, they stick. And so it was in the many locales that we lived in. In our New Jersey community, we were like one big family. We partied and shared many events. After moving to Poughkeepsie, our past friendships were still important to us. When it was Helen and Morty's 25th anniversary in 1979, they decided to spend it at a hotel just off Central Park in Manhattan and enjoy the city. We resolved to share a part of it and meet them at their hotel.

What do you bring a couple for their silver anniversary? Browsing through a store, we were attracted to a sculpture of an "ape holding the skull of man," a take-off on the Darwin theory of "man contemplating our relationship to apes." We brought it to Helen and Morty at their hotel. Morty made fun of the gift. We weren't sure whether he was joking or not. He brought it down to the restaurant in the hotel and placed it as a centerpiece on the table. The next time we visited them in New Jersey, we came with chachka of a "monkey humorously jumping rope." "Why did you buy this?" Morty asked.

We said, "It's a gift for the ape." That became a joke between us, and now, for over forty years, we've been sending each other "monkey" cards for our birthdays and anniversaries. True to our beliefs, maintaining friendships was important to us. Mitch and Sue moved from Yorktowne in New Jersey, to Houston, and subsequently to Atlanta. After learning to fly, Mitch shared a partnership with other fellows who had purchased a small four-seat plane. While we were living in Poughkeepsie, Mitch and Sue came to visit us with their sons, in their small plane. We stood on the tarmac as this plane flew into an executive airport near us and taxied towards us. It was mind-boggling for us, like something out of a comic book, to be having them fly in just for lunch, for our reunion, before they headed out to Massachusetts. It was a delightful interlude with two dear friends.

Unfortunately, a decade or more later, while we were living in Tampa, we got a call that Mitch crashed the plane in Atlanta, and he and Sue were killed. They were heading from a small airport to the international airport for some repairs when, according to other pilots, wind gusts pulled them off the approaching runway, and they crashed in a cemetery. At their funeral, it was difficult to watch their two coffins being lowered into the earth.

Like I said, when you're my friend, you are my friend forever. In all the moves we made I always kept that promise. Friendships are an important part of the fabric of your life. Your continued contact with those you care about, and who care about you, helps to make you whole.

SNAPSHOT 26

SO I AIN'T ELEGANT?

L iving in New Jersey, we frequently went into New York City with our little family for entertainment. One time we went to a Chinese restaurant, a type of cuisine I always enjoyed. After we finished our meal and left the restaurant, we walked a few blocks to retrieve our car, and return home. I started feeling discomfort in my upper body and stopped to buy some aspirin.

When we got in the car and crossed into New Jersey on the turnpike, I began loosening my garments because I started feeling pressure in my chest and was nauseous.

Paul pulled the car over to the side of the road. I was frightened of what I was experiencing.

The police arrived and asked if an ambulance was necessary.

After I regurgitated and sat for a while, I began to feel better. I just wanted to go home.

The next day, Paul went to his allergist and shared my episode with the doctor. The doctor said he knew what happened. I had ingested a lump of MSG, instead of the usual powder form of that additive in the Chinese food. My body reacted to it. He said others had experienced the same problem, so he was familiar with the symptoms. I still eat in Chinese restaurants, but thankfully, have never had another problem related to MSG.

The Waldorf Astoria was the most elegant and famous hotel in New York City. When IBM invites you to a dinner there, it's a special event. In the late 1960s, Paul and I were looking forward to dinner at the Waldorf, having never been there before. We dressed accordingly, in our finest attire.

When we arrived, many IBMers were in the lobby, outside the dining hall, drinking at the bar before going in to dinner. The chairman of IBM was a teetotaler and liquor was forbidden at company affairs. We entered the ballroom and were seated at a table of eight, with other couples, one of who was an IBM salesman. We learned later that each table had an IBM salesman seated with them. We introduced ourselves and indulged in light conversation before dinner began and then all hell broke loose.

The Waldorf had its own unique format for serving the meal. Each waiter, dressed in a tuxedo, took care of his table. "DING," a bell rang and the relish tray was carried around the table. As it was offered to me, I tried to remove a stalk of celery from a bunch on the tray.

The waiter whispered to me, "Take the whole thing."

I decided to pass on that generous offer.

"DING." Our appetizer plates were removed before I could eat the appetizer.

"DING." Soup was served.

"DING." The soup bowls were removed.

But, alas, the waiter had to come back for my spoon, which I had not left in the bowl. An extra trip for our waiter.

A microphone announcement suggested we eat our salads

which were waiting alongside our dinner plates. The waiter, apparently annoyed with me, switched the salad because I took it from the wrong side of my dinner plate. Paul didn't eat salad at that time anyway, so he did not mind that I was eating his.

"DING." The salad plates were removed.

Obviously, my best etiquette was not on display.

"DING." The entrees were served. I enjoyed it, but can't remember what it was. I ate it without making another faux pas.

"DING." The entrée plates were removed.

"DING." Dessert was served. I am looking at this cream stuffed crusted shell. I tap the hard crust and decide I'm not going to indulge because as the evening is going, it would probably fly right off my plate.

While Paul and I are giggling at the weirdness of the dinner, at a table next to us, a dessert goes flying into the air. I couldn't believe it. I thought it was going to be me doing that. A lot of giggling followed that.

I was just relishing my hot cup of coffee. "DING." The dishes were cleared and the speeches began.

My passport to the Waldorf Astoria was revoked. Fine by me.

SNAPSHOT 27

MY BIG BROTHER, MURRAY

My brother Murray

My brother, Murray, was a positive part of my life. As I said previously, he was very good to me, in many ways, as a big brother. We were not alike at all, but we made sure that the love we felt for each other was always present. Because of the five-year difference in age, we didn't get involved in activities together, but he was always there if I needed him.

Murray was very focused on success, and his pursuit of educational excellence enabled him to follow that path. He was the controller of a large trucking company. His success was honored in "Who's Who In America," a highly respected publication. But he was much more than just a business success.

When his youngest son, Eliot, had his Bar Mitzvah, at thirteen years old, Murray paid to bring his whole family to Chicago for this special event. He flew Mom, Dad, Paul, and me, with our two daughters, from Brooklyn. He also paid for his wife Ruthie's mom and brother Jack's family to fly from Brooklyn, her sister's family from Los Angeles, and her other brother's family from Seattle. Not only did he pay for all those flights, but he also took care of our hotel charges. It was a momentous weekend for all of us thanks to Murray's incredible generosity.

What also made Murray special was that he made sure to put us in touch with the right connections when my daughter Debra needed medical help.

When, in later years, Murray's company sailed their sixty-foot yacht down to Miami from Chicago, he invited Paul and me, not only to stay at the Doral, a prestigious hotel in Miami, but to also sail on the yacht to the Bahamas, with Ruthie and another couple. We tried deep sea fishing, and that was a lot of fun. The captain and his mate made sure we were successful, helping us with our catches. The captain was perched on an upper level, and as we took turns with the fishing pole, he yelled, "Get ready! Here come the fish!" "Bam!" We hooked it. I caught some pretty large fish and had to figure out how to rein them in. We then traveled to Bimini and laid out our large fish on the ground, it impressed the other fishermen. After wandering around the island, we sailed to Freeport. Staying in a hotel was a welcome departure from sleeping on board. As I stood in the shower, I could still feel myself swaying. Back on the yacht, Paul kept catching barracuda which were thrown back in. Toward the end of the trip, he was more successful and pulled out a large Mahi Mahi. When that fish came out of the water, it was a beautiful iridescent color, but turned gray afterwards. The Captain asked if Paul wanted it mounted, but Paul responded, "I want it on my fork." So the Captain cooked a delicious dinner for the whole group. Sadly, I did not get to eat it because I got seasick. Murray caught a very large Wahoo, which he had mounted and placed in his office.

After many years with his company, Murray decided to go into partnership with a co-worker. Of course, they believed working together would be a terrific deal. They set it up in Muncie, Indiana. Unfortunately, the venture failed and the business folded. They each put a lot of money into the business, which was all lost. My brother ended up working with his son, Paul, who had a trucking company, but much smaller, in New Jersey. Sometimes in life, you get too smart, and think you can do anything you pursue. Sadly, it doesn't always work that way.

Murray made a lot of bad choices and his world fell apart. The failure of the partnership, messing with the books, in collusion with his son, and ending up in jail for a short time took him down. He went into business and personal bankruptcies. He was only able to keep his home and a car. Previous to this, he crashed his car on the New Jersey Turnpike. The auto was demolished. Thankfully, my brother was not badly hurt.

Murray did not follow rules. He refused to wear a seat belt when it was initially ordered into law. He told me that on one trip, driving from Chicago to New York, he was pulled over three times for speeding. The officers took his credit card and swiped it right there on the highway. You would think he would have learned his lesson after the first stop. Not Murray.

In the community where he lived, Murray started doing taxes for truckers. They passed his name around and he got more clients. Even then, he was making bad choices, and he would call me for financial help on a few occasions. I was always at the end of that phone line for him. I always tried to be there when he needed me.

One day, he called to tell me that although he was the executor of our parents' will, he had to be removed because everything he received would have to go to the IRS. So, I became the executor but told him I would split with him whatever was given to me. I followed through with that promise because he was the best brother for me. I loved his caring nature.

It's amazing how you can go through life, being on top of the world, and then fall into a hole.

Murray had a few heart attacks and did not take care of himself medically. Unfortunately, he died a very painful death in 2014. Gangrene attacked his intestines. I will always miss my big brother. Whatever else happened to him, he always loved and cared about me. And I loved him too.

SNAPSHOT 28

1976: THE ENCOUNTER

1976 was a year of big changes for us. We were leaving our first home in Yorktowne and moving back to New York State, this time in Poughkeepsie. But there was something else we did that made a big change in us.

That July, we went on a miraculous weekend to Marriage Encounter. There we discovered a new insight into Paul and Sandy. It was a view into something we didn't realize we were missing in our relationship.

Our daughter Judy was in camp, and Debra had moved out into her own apartment by the New Jersey shore. We were alone.

The adventure began as a mysterious weekend at a hotel where we did not know what to expect. A team consisting of a Rabbi, his wife, and two other couples greeted us. They would be the ones leading us down a path to discover more about each other. We were already married 22 years. How much more could we learn about each other?

We were sequestered into a room that had no TV and no telephone; no other communication except with each other.

Communication is the key to this magic encounter. The

team of six persons presented various subjects for us to think about. They wanted us to write down our feelings relative to each presentation while we were in separate rooms. Then, as husband and wife, in privacy, get back to each other to read and discuss our individual responses. The subjects delved deeper and deeper about our feelings for each other. We started out writing for about a half hour each time. As the subjects became more complex, some took as much as ninety minutes to address.

Some were very difficult. One example: "How would you feel if you lost each other?" That was very emotional and I wondered how much I could write for ninety minutes allotted to that question.

Well, it just pours out of you, and you write and write. You realize that without each other, you would lose so much: the sweetness, the soft touch, and tenderness. Without your partner, you would look out on a wasteland devoid of color and music. When we completed the segment, we were both crying as we tried to read each other's responses. We grasped each other, the emotions overwhelming. Suddenly, we saw notes that had been passed under our door. They were from other couples who had been here previous weekends. The notes made it clear that these couples experienced the same feelings we now had. We were touched by their caring.

We traveled down into the depths of our relationship, reaching into the foundation, building an even stronger love for each other. We had buried our feelings down in the earth, but the subjects they asked us to discuss brought our emotions back to the surface. As we continued on this path, the subjects got lighter for us and the joy of our relationship took greater hold. We pulled away layers of who we were and rediscovered what we mean to each other. These were love letters we wrote for each other, discovering new ways to communicate our thoughts and feelings. We learned we could put so much more into our communications when we write. It gives us time to think unlike when we are in a conversation. One-on-one verbal communication doesn't always bring forth the deep and honest thoughts that writing allows.

As we revealed to each other more about ourselves, the reaction was "Really. I didn't know that!" We kept surprising each other but knew that whatever we wrote, we could trust our life partner. That's the secret of Marriage Encounter. They want couples who are married for a while and know that their marriage is good. They want couples that trust and care about each other's feelings. If a marriage is not on solid ground, this kind of encounter can be torn apart.

I did not know how much more I could love Paul. That weekend was better than my honeymoon. We ended the magic by all the couples joining in a circle and holding on to each other singing:

"There's a new world somewhere
They call the Promised Land
And I'll be there some day
If you will hold my hand
I still need you there beside me
No matter what I do
For I know I'll never find another you.

There is always someone
For each of us they say
And you'll be my someone

Forever and a day
I could search the whole world over
Until my life is through
But I know I'll never find another you.

It's a long, long journey
So stay by my side
When I walk through a storm
You'll be my guide
Be my guide.

If they gave me a fortune
My pleasure would be small
I could lose it all tomorrow
And never mind at all
But if I should lose your love, dear
I don't know what I'd do
For I know I'll never find another you.

When that weekend ended, we knew that "I'll lean on you and you lean on me, and we'll be okay" was all we needed. We remembered that we still had our original letters we wrote when Paul was in the Marines, when we found each other. After we got home, we pulled them out of the attic. We sat together on the couch and read them aloud to each other. It was a wonderful climax to an enchanting and loving weekend. I never forgot it. Neither did Paul.

SNAPSHOT 29

1976: WINTER IN POUGHKEEPSIE

In 1976, America celebrated the Bicentennial. It was 200 years since the founding of a new democracy, called the United States of America. There were celebrations everywhere on July 4, 1976. I remember lots of ships from that colonial era sailing up the Hudson River in New York. It was quite an awesome sight.

Good things were also happening in South Africa as apartheid came to an end.

With the transfer of Paul to Poughkeepsie, which was about 100 miles north of New York City, a new episode in our life began. The move made us feel like immigrants coming to a new country that was foreign to us. It was an IBM town for the most part. It seemed like each person we met worked for IBM. Our circle of friends, except for one, were all IBMers.

Poughkeepsie was along the Hudson River, a beautiful town with lots of scenery to enjoy. Paul's office was right along the river, and he told me that many times, during lunch hours, he would sit outside and meditate, enjoying his new surroundings.

But it was very cold in the winter months, something we weren't used to. The first month that we moved in was

November. I recall telling my husband after day after day of below-freezing temperatures, "I'm not getting out of bed until it hits 0." That's how cold it felt to us.

After many more months at work, Paul's manager asked, "How do you like Poughkeepsie?"

Paul answered, "Spring is beautiful. The fall colors are spectacular, and summers are okay, but the other 8 months...."

In 1976, we purchased a new Toyota Camry in New Jersey. We were bringing it back to our new home in Poughkeepsie, New York. Paul had a visit with his ophthalmologist while we were visiting in our former neighborhood and his eyes had been dilated, so he asked me to drive.

It was December and we had a lot of inclement weather. Snow was pushed aside on the interstate. I was moving along at a steady pace in the left lane. As I came out from under an overpass, I hit a patch of ice and the car started to slide. Remembering the proper procedure in the manuals, I turned in the direction of the skid.

Paul was stunned.

The car turned to the right and was sliding across three lanes of the highway. I hit a snowbank and landed on the top. It happened so fast that I did not know how the other cars got around me.

When we got our wits about us, Paul and I determined we were okay.

A policeman approached the car. "Are you alright?" he asked.

"Yes Sir," I replied.

"What happened?" he asked.

"I don't know. You tell me since you witnessed it." The whole incident was a blur to me. With not much time to think, I just reacted reflexively.

The car was towed off the snowbank and we decided it was drivable.

Paul's eyes cleared up immediately, and he continued the drive home.

SNAPSHOT 30

1976: TO MOVE OR NOT TO MOVE?

The house was larger than our previous one and we planted a lot of colorful bushes, notably rhododendrons. They were delightful to behold in June with their large pink flowers in bloom.

When the weather cooperated, we set out exploring the surrounding area and enjoyed the adventure. There were magnificent mountains and freshwater lakes that we swam in. We even brought their fresh water home to enjoy drinking. It was beautiful vistas that we thoroughly enjoyed. Life is not measured by the number of breaths we take, but by the moments that take our breath away. We had many such experiences.

Paul was happy at his new job, which was only four miles from our home. In jest, he would say, "What a bummer! I had to stop for a traffic light."

At a company party, I met a fellow who was talking about having had to move many times. The company joke was that the acronym, IBM, stood for, "I've been moved."

I asked this man, "How do you handle all the moves?"

He responded, "Actually, I have no regrets. I tell myself, I wouldn't have met all these nice people and accumulated new friends without all the moves."

I thought it was a positive outlook, a great way to look at life's opportunities.

I found my way with new opportunities too. I was selling Avon and joined an organization called Women's American ORT. This group focused on supporting depressed areas in Africa, teaching them skills to improve their lives. In our local area, I hosted a radio program with others where we interviewed people working at different jobs. I asked them what they liked and disliked about their jobs and instructed them to be very candid. They were dentists, plumbers, electricians, pharmacists, and more. The object was to enlighten teenagers so that they could use that knowledge to plan their future.

The only problem was that it was on a Sunday morning at 9:00 AM, when teenagers were still asleep.

After our wonderful experience with Marriage Encounter the previous summer, we found three other couples who had taken the program as well. We formed a group, and once a month took turns as hosts, choosing the subject, and being presenters for the evening. We all got insight into each other as we talked about how we all felt about these subjects. Learning from our experience, Paul and I continued to write to each other when a subject came up that we wanted to discuss. It really helped.

During this time, each of our daughters met their future husbands. They married in a beautiful setting at an inn along the Hudson River. It was a joy to see them find their love and branch out and discover their own way in life.

After their marriages: Judy & Ron, Debra & Mike

I made changes as well. I decided to become a travel agent. I had been very content with my life, but the only thing missing was fulfilling my desire to see the world. With training as an agent, I set out in that direction.

After 5 years in the cold, Paul was ready to go to a warmer climate. He asked for a transfer to Florida.

SNAPSHOT 31

1982: SUNNY DAYS

Welcome to Tampa. It's 1982. The first thing we see is a truck driving in front of us with a Confederate flag, and a gun rack holding two rifles across from each other. Where have we moved to? Where do we Yankees from the northlands belong?

We built a single-level house in Tampa, and we're so content with the design making it very comfortable to live in. We built two homes previously, but this one was unique. In its smaller 1,660 square footage, there are so many good features. We didn't know the square footage of the previous homes, but they were larger.

It's very deceptive looking at the house from the street. You see a two-car garage, but the rest of the house is behind it, except for one bedroom set back and peeking out on the side. We changed the three bedrooms into two large bedrooms. The dining room is in the middle of the house with room to seat twelve persons easily. Next to it is a built-in lighted bar with a sink and storage area. The living room is a step down with room for two couches and a love seat. Plus, it has a fireplace. We wondered, "Who needs a fireplace in Florida?" but it came with the package. Throughout the house, the commercial carpeting held up very well for twenty-two years, and when the house was sold, it still looked new. The kitchen and dinette were spacious with a washer and dryer concealed behind doors.

Now that we live in Florida, we decided to put in a freeform, in-the-ground pool because we did not have much land. What a pleasure that was. Sometimes at night with dim lighting, we'd just swim naked, until a two-story house was built next door. We planned pool parties for our new friends, but many came without swimsuits because they had their own pools. So, the parties were indoors and outdoors, and we just had fun. Luckily, we already had IBM friends who had lived here for two years. They introduced us to many couples.

Pool parties in Tampa

93

Our home was across the street from a golf course, which thrilled us because we had been golfing since the 1970s. However, I was never an expert at it, even after lessons. I decided to approach the golf pro, who asked, "What's your problem?"

I replied, "I can't count that high."

His retort was, "Are you in a tournament?"

"No."

"Then why are you counting?"

Paul and I never counted again. We would just go out and have fun. That was 1982, and here I am, in 2020, playing golf, and not counting.

SNAPSHOT 32

AN ACTIVE LIFE

P aul was a half hour away from his office and was told that his hours were flexible. He, therefore, planned to go in early and leave work early, so that he could be home by 5:00 PM to play golf when we want to. The problem is that in the summer, it often rains around 5:00 PM, and in the winter months, it gets dark early.

Some days, as an alternative to golf in the evenings, we'd drive out to the Gulf Coast, about an hour away, and watch the sunset on the beach. The colors were spectacular, and you felt as though a good day just ended and you were ready for another dawning. My daughter Judy and her husband Ron recently bought a house along the Gulf Coast, and they get to watch this beautiful sunset every night.

The IBM building was a block from an NFL football stadium for the Buccaneers. We were excited to get season tickets. They were not accessible in the New York area because people would not give up their seats. They handed them down to family members or friends. We totally enjoyed all the games and yelled and moaned with our seatmates.

We had a great time living in Tampa. Disney World was a

one-and-a-half-hour drive. EPCOT is the park we enjoyed the most. When our family came to visit, we all would go to Disney World, and it became a special treat for all of us.

In 1982, cell phones came into use. The popular film E.T. debuted and the David Letterman's late-night show began.

I found a job as a Travel Agent and the world opened up for me. I did not have set hours but arranged to be an "outside agent," so that I could travel at any time and make sure that I could visit my daughters in Colorado and New York. Paul had six weeks off a year, and nothing held us back. I had my own clientele, which I built up over time. I also had the use of the office, with my own desk, as well as access to all their equipment: computers and reference materials. I made my own appointments, sometimes meeting clients after hours, using my own key to the office. It was a perfect setup; flexible hours and a 50/50 split in commissions. Even when I was out of town, my boss took care of my clients.

I never had such an opportunity and the agency owners sent me for training whenever there was a change in the computer system. The best part was when pamphlets were passed to me that piqued my interest as a possible destination. I worked it out with my sweetheart and off we went.

Most of the time, as a Travel Agent, I got wonderful discounts for myself and Paul on tours as well as flights. The airlines gave us special treatment. Sometimes, if there was a first-class seat available on the plane, they gave it to us. We visited all over Europe, the South Pacific, and Asia. Asia was our favorite destination because the culture was so different. We also loved cruising and were on more than twenty ship voyages.

In 1986, a performing arts center was built in Tampa, which was comparable in size to the Kennedy Center in Washington,

D.C. We took advantage of the Broadway selections which came from touring companies direct from Broadway in New York City. We also loved the POPS concerts that were offered. It almost felt like we were back in the Northeast with new cultural opportunities.

Paul and I played tennis with two female players. The losers would have to buy the bagels for breakfast. Paul was never uncomfortable playing with just women, but he had another game with guys.

Another activity we loved was being a part of a team that built sandcastles on the beach on Treasure Island. The sand sculptures were incredible. They were very creative, built around a theme, and the public came to see them. We sprayed starch on them, so they held up against inclement weather and were able to be viewed for a length of time. That was really "fun in the sun."

SNAPSHOT 33

THE BAT MITZVAH

W e joined a Jewish Reform Temple. I decided that I wanted to have a Bat Mitzvah, which girls usually have at thirteen, but I was fifty. I wanted to do this for a very long time, ever since we had our first temple in New Jersey, and others attained that goal.

I was in a group of three men and two other women. It took a lot of training and I had to study Hebrew, but I was ready to tackle it.

On my big day, as I looked out at my family in the audience, and saw my friends, I feel uplifted that I made this choice. When my daughters accomplished it at age thirteen, it wasn't their choice. It was expected of them. I was proud that I made this choice on my own.

My Mom, Dad, and other relatives were also there. Sadly, my mother died four months later. That taught me to always celebrate your high moments because they can be snuffed out like a lit match.

I felt as if I had scaled to the top of a mountain, looking out on the horizons I could still reach. The world was mine, but I did not know if I could manage it. I learned that it's these small happenings that make life so spectacular. This shy girl from Brooklyn, living in city housing, had reached as high as the clouds. How much higher could I get? We found a wonderful city to live in. We had made terrific friends and still kept in touch with friends from the past. Our family was growing with four grandchildren. Paul's salary was rising and he was happy at work. What more can I ask for?

But there's always a catch, something that comes out of nowhere to challenge you.

I was diagnosed with a rare malignancy.

I was devastated. The ground had suddenly opened up and I was falling in.

Paul kept trying to encourage me. He gave me pep talks about our future and all the great trips we were going to take together. I did not think I was going to live that long.

I had to have radiation treatment at Moffitt Hospital…

After my radiation treatment was over, I volunteered to be in some drug studies, but I was told there were none for me because only thirty percent of people survive this cancer. How do I handle that? A friend suggested that I find humor in my predicament, surround myself with laughter. I went out and bought a book of laugh-out-loud humor. I would read it and burst into laughter. I tried to focus on humor and the positives of my life. It helped me get through. I could not have done it without Paul pushing me on and holding my hand.

Many years later, my friend, Betty, had the same rare cancer and she didn't survive. I am grateful that I am with the thirty percent survival group, because it's thirty-one years later, and here I am writing about my life.

Paul retired from IBM, not because he planned it. IBM was downsizing and as he was with the company for 35 years, he is among the chosen ones.

Retirement was an adjustment for Paul, but he worked it out, finding buddies at the gym with whom to hang out. He also arranged with other IBM retirees to teach computer technology to seniors at the local college.

One always has to turn the page in life, but together we learned to grow with each change. There's a saying, "Strength is what we gain from the difficulties we survive." I believe that.

SNAPSHOT 34

2003: DISNEY WORLD FOR ADULTS?

The Villages, Florida. What a fantastic retirement community. It is now the largest in the world. Paul and I moved for the lifestyle, which is unlike any other retirement facility.

While we lived in Tampa, we decided to move to a retirement community. We arrived in The Villages to look around. Who would have believed there was such a location? It was very hard to resist. There is no comparison anywhere else. Actually, it is often called "Disney World for Seniors."

It is interesting how they encouraged you to buy here. We took a bus that toured around the community. The host's commentary made you feel you had to live here. Before we got on the bus, the host took a picture of Paul and me sitting in front of a sign that said, "Solomon Drive." We bought into the dream in 2003.

Taking the tour at The Villages

Instead of downsizing, which we had planned to do, we built a 1,926 square foot home because the model was so appealing. An additional attraction was that we were told it would be completed in three months, and to the day, it was done. Friends of ours that bought into a retirement complex in Lake Worth, Florida waited a year for the completion.

Our house has three bedrooms: two on one side, and one very large one on the other. The feature that we liked best was that there was a tiled pathway and each room was accessible from it, so that you never had to walk through any room to get to another. Roman columns segregate each section of the living room and dining room, and a patio with a sliding door lies beyond. The kitchen and dinette are a large area, and we're so comfortable as we were in our previous home in Tampa.

This will be the last house that we build.

The Villages is eighty miles north of Tampa, so we could still visit our friends and family, and we continued our subscription at the Performing Arts Center and the football stadium. How perfect is that?

You have the option to use your car or a golf cart to navigate around this huge complex. The golf cart was great for Paul as he began losing some sight and, after many years, had to give up his driver's license. He could still make use of the facilities here and not feel as if he lost his independence. The golf cart's highest speed was twenty miles an hour and he traversed mostly on separate golf cart paths.

There are fifty-three golf courses in The Villages. In addition, there are over 3,000 clubs in 100 recreation centers, all of which are available to every resident. Free entertainment is provided every night in three different town squares, comprised of retail shops and restaurants. Each night, there's a band for our dancing pleasure. With over one hundred restaurants, we have never eaten out so much in our lives.

After a few months of taking advantage of the clubs, which are run by volunteers, and enjoying the entertainment, we decided this was the best move we ever made. The amenity fee, which we pay monthly, came to around $100.00, but in 2020 is now $146.00. All the facilities and golf courses are free for our use, whenever we want for that fee.

The amenity fee also covers the infrastructure of the area. With all the landscaping it looks like we're living in a park because it's so beautiful and well maintained. The plantings are done quarterly, and the colors continually change, a technicolor for your eyes.

My boss at the travel agency in Tampa wanted me to continue

working in The Villages. She said she would set up the computer system in my home, and with all the retirees here, I could do a lot of business. She was right. I could be successful, but I told her that I was going into retirement.

I found a great many activities to keep me busy here. A foreign film club, as well as vintage films, are offered in the recreation centers, and that has been fun. My most unusual choice has been a scrapbooking club. You gather photos, add commentary, and decorate each page. It was a very creative activity which I thoroughly enjoyed. Initially, I made a scrapbook for each of my grandchildren from their birth into their twenties. When they were completed, I gave a scrapbook to each of them. Each book took a year to complete because they were very detailed. When they were finished, I made two scrapbooks of the trips we took around the world. Lastly, "The Story of Us," the life of Sandy and Paul.

Walking around the room and viewing all the other creations that people were making gave me many ideas. I love this club and consider it a highlight of my involvement in this community. But you can also add in golf, bocce, as well as bridge, mahjongg, and card games. There's a club here for every type of music, sport, craft, and exercise.

The Villages community is a melting pot, where residents are from all across the country and globe. Every state has a club and every village formed its club. There are clubs for every ethnicity, such as Italian, Jewish, Irish, and African-American. Every holiday brings out a celebration in the town squares, complete with parades and bands.

Paul's and my days and nights were full. We participated in most activities together, but not everything held both our interests. Paul went off to the gym and the computer club that he enjoyed. To enhance and stimulate our minds, we participated in different educational classes at the high school. These fun courses later moved to the recreation centers.

When I said that we have over 3,000 clubs, it is due to the fact that The Villages has grown much larger over the seventeen years that I have lived here. When we arrived in 2003, there were thirty-three thousand residents in this community. Now, there are over one hundred thirty thousand residents as The Villages owners continue to purchase land further south, building and building new villages. This small town has become a metropolis. While I love it still, I think it has lost some of the closeness of the community we used to feel.

We made a lot of new friends in The Villages. Many friends were from a Jewish club we joined. The members had begun the formation of a new temple, and before we knew it, we became active in the group. By the end of 2006, the building was completed and Temple Shalom was born.

I began putting together trips to Orlando for the temple, which is east of us, as well as Tampa and St. Petersburg, which are south. Over the years, I built up a following of residents who especially love to go to the Performing Arts Center in Tampa. I run two or three trips a year to see shows coming directly from Broadway.

The growth of the number of congregants in the Temple was amazing. After Paul died, I needed a purpose to continue my life and overcome my grief. I ran for President and was elected in 2018. It was a challenge, but I persevered. The temple was in disarray after having a Rabbi who was not the best fit for our congregation. There was a lot of anger. But I learned that everyone you meet deserves to be greeted with a smile. Dealing with some of my board members was more difficult. I remembered the saying, "Diplomacy is telling people to go to Hell in such a way that they ask for directions." I listened and tried not to react, and it worked well. When it did not, I would not let it upset me. After two years, I let someone else take over. Overall, it was a successful experience when I saw that congregants were more content with their surroundings. A new Rabbi definitely helped. I was glad I played an important part in the history of the temple, even if at times it was difficult.

In 2020, we were dealing with the worst pandemic in the history of the world. Some compared it to the Black Plague in the Middle Ages. Thankfully, vaccines were developed, with more on the way. We can look forward to a "new normal" once again.

So many other events have occurred during this time, both sad and joyful. Deadly wildfires erupted from California to Washington state, killing many people and ruining lives. Supreme Court Justice Ruth Bader Ginsburg died, a great woman who also happened to be Jewish. Her influence on the Supreme Court impressed me.

Best of all, Joe Biden was elected our new President.

SNAPSHOT 35

PRINCE CHARMING

The Happy Couple As Time Goes By

How do you measure a relationship? My husband, Paul, was my life. He was my soulmate. The forces that brought us together were magical. You could say it was like a fairytale because he truly was my Prince Charming. How could I know at the young age of sixteen that a pen pal connection would change my life forever? We often wondered how two people could fit together so well. Our likes and dislikes were exactly the same.

We just enjoyed being with each other in all aspects of living, whether in music, sports, entertainment, and sex. He was a very loving husband, and his biggest pleasure was to make me happy. I always responded by wanting to do the same for him. Through our ups and downs, which always are a part of life, we grew closer to each other. There were times when tears and sadness consumed me, and his caresses and understanding helped me rise above it. He shed tears and cried on my shoulder when it became necessary to ease his pain. Mostly we laughed.

Paul had a great sense of humor and was a terrific joke teller. Over the years, he could tell me the same jokes, and I laughed and laughed, having no memory of hearing it before. I was definitely a great audience. He encouraged me to get over my shyness, reach out in all directions, and have confidence in all my endeavors. As I began to trust in my decisions, Paul would try and listen to my opinions. When we argued, either agree or disagree, we were always willing to work together.

Paul's warmth permeated throughout our lives, and he made friends easily. No matter where we lived, Paul made the transition well, because he was friendly. Many times he would just get up to be a part of a routine that was being performed by a comedian, just for the joy of participating. He loved to dance, sometimes making up his own steps, but as long as he was having fun, no one noticed.

We painted and wallpapered together, sometimes giggling when it wasn't exactly going right. Jigsaw puzzles were the challenges we enjoyed together, and I've continued doing them to this day.

Paul loved to sing even though he was tone-deaf and couldn't hold a note. Our little temple in New Jersey had a choir, and whenever they were looking for more volunteers, Paul's hand always went up. It was a joke we dealt with for many years. When we were sadly moving elsewhere, the choir leader made sure to make him a part of the last service. We all watched him beaming as he sang along.

Our lives changed drastically in June 2014 when, thinking Paul showed symptoms of a stroke, I took him to the hospital. None of the medical personnel could come up with an answer to his problems because it was not a stroke. In an instant, he had forgotten how to swallow or even use a fork when I served dinner. The doctors sent him to the Mayo Clinic. After a week of tests, they determined that physically he was fine but was in a deep depression which manifested itself physically.

I did not see it coming. What could have caused this?

SNAPSHOT 36

BRING BACK MY PRINCE

The week prior to bringing Paul to the hospital, my brother, Murray, died. But they really were not that close, even though they were the same age, only six days apart. Paul told me that he did not feel the urge to go to the funeral which surprised me, so I went with my daughter, Debra. I never found out why Paul did not want to go. I did not know he was in a depression at the time.

When I returned from the funeral, after only two nights away, Paul told me that after a bath, he was sitting on the toilet drying himself when he fell and landed on the floor. He said he hit his head on the edge of the tub but thought he was okay.

The next few days, I noticed Paul doing some strange things. He decided to trim a bush which our gardeners had already taken care of previously. I then saw he was at the computer, printing the same document over and over. On the fourth day after I got home, thinking he was showing the symptoms of a stroke, I decided to take him to the hospital. When I served dinner that night, I saw he had forgotten how to swallow or use a fork. I thought his behaviors were caused by his accident.

None of the doctors could come up with an answer to what

was causing Paul's problems, but said it was not a stroke. The doctors sent him to rehab to help him with his swallowing of food. After a few days, he was sent to the Mayo Clinic for further evaluation. They did a battery of tests for a week and determined that physically, he was fine. They told me he was in a deep depression, which manifested itself with physical symptoms. I never saw it coming.

Following many doctors' orders, Paul was placed in hospitals and then rehabs for seven months. He was uncooperative with any help offered. He even talked of suicide, so they moved his bed next to the nurses' station and monitored him. Nobody seemed to know what was happening to my husband. We wanted to help him, but he only wanted to die. It was breaking my heart. I felt helpless.

I thought I was taking care of him, going from doctor to doctor, facility to facility, each giving conflicting suggestions of what to do next. At one point, when he was in the hospital again because of his elevated coumadin level, his doctor suggested I put him in rehab for three months because it was covered by Medicare, and so he could regain his strength and get therapy for depression. It seemed the right decision at the time, but Paul still refused to cooperate. I was frustrated and did not know how to handle all this, especially when he would not talk to me. I also was not aware the doctor was an investor in this rehab. I discovered that only after Paul was placed there.

Paul became incontinent and couldn't take care of himself. I was extremely concerned and tried to encourage him, but he still would not talk to me. He was angry, and psychologists were no help. No psychologist could explain to me what my husband was feeling. I did not need specific answers but give me an idea of what was going on. I wanted to take him home but could not because I was unable to take care of him. I did not know what to do.

Over many months, I tried to understand what initially brought it all on. I felt as if I had lost a part of me, the anchor that was my heart, my being, though he was right in front of me. Could it be the frustration of slowly losing his sight over many years? Was it the inability to do what he wanted to do on the computer, something he had used most of his life? Could it be his family history because his mom attempted suicide? Could it be his brain chemistry? Was it one thing that set him off, or a bunch of little things adding up to something big? He went from a happy-go-lucky guy to a lost soul in what seemed a matter of minutes.

Realizing again I couldn't take care of him myself, I reluctantly placed Paul in an assisted living facility, where he continued to be uncooperative.

After a few months, one day, as I did every day, I came to visit my husband. When I saw him, he said he could not see me. Overnight, his vision had diminished severely. I decided I would bring him home with twenty-four-hour care. That was the best decision I made during those seven horrible months. The hell with the costs. He was now getting one-on-one care from nurses and aides, with no need to ring a bell and wait for assistance. He was home.

Paul soon began to talk to me again. He expressed his feeling that I had abandoned him. I was shocked and bewildered because I believed I was doing everything possible for him. His view was different.

After almost a year, because we had so little time together, I decided to take Paul on a 'date' once a week, to a folk music club in The Villages. He realized he did not need to see in order to be part of the performance. He could enjoy the music and sing along with everyone. Eventually, we bought a tambourine and he loved to join in keeping beat with the guitarists. Slowly, he started to come back to life again. After a year of home care assistance, I dismissed the medical staff, first at night and then daytime.

During the next year and a half, we went to as many clubs as I could find where Paul did not need his sight. The Villages has many choices for participation and I searched them out.

The VA was a wonderful source of support. Through their "Blind Veterans Association," a team would come and visit Paul, bringing him different aids and apparatus to help him regain independence. It began to make him more confident and realize, as the VA team always said, "You can do anything you want, but you just have to do it differently."

We began to smile again. It lifted the stone in my heart, as I began to feel my husband coming back into my life. I asked Paul if he could tell me what brought on the depression, but he said he did not know. I was hopeful it was in our past.

SNAPSHOT 37

AN INSPIRATIONAL JOURNEY TOGETHER

As I reflect on the past, we learned to adapt to all situations, and to each other. My dear Paul had a momentous change in his life when he fell into a deep depression that affected him physically. Losing his sight was a major factor. As I went through it with him, my life changed as well. I had to adapt to living alone without him for eight months and dealing with his trauma. When he came home, and we worked with twenty-four-hour care, I believe he realized how much he was loved, and slowly emerged from darkness to light, despair to hope.

The night crew was at his beck and call, retired nurses from the neighborhood who showed their warmth and humor to Paul, so he could get through the nights.

The day crew was two men, one a retired nurse and the other a massage therapist. They became buddies and made him feel comfortable with their male chit-chat. One was a former Marine and the other was young enough to be Paul's son. After a year, when Paul came back to life, and after I discharged the aides, we began to live as husband and wife again. Despite his loss of sight, being nearly blind, not being able to see my face anymore, he was learning to accept his situation and developing independence.

The Blind Veterans Association was a major contributor to Paul's care. During monthly visits, their members brought him different items to encourage him to cope in his new world: a talking watch to tell him the time; a recorder to remind him of a need; a sensor to put on a glass so that he could pour liquid. It beeped when the glass was full. They put a button set at 30-second intervals on the microwave. When he pushed the button three times, he could make his cup of tea. They brought a device where he could put a document or magazine on a tray, and an arm with a camera would rise, record it and read back the text to him. They set up Alexa, a device from Amazon that played music when he asked, and helped him enjoy a football game once again. With Alexa connected to a local sports radio station, a voice announced the game plays, while I watched it on TV. We could whoop and holler at the plays together. The VA set up a button on the phone connecting to my cell phone if Paul needed to reach me when I was out doing errands. They connected him to the library to get books on tape for his enjoyment, and he became a voracious listener to the many stories available.

Paul exercised to get his strength back, and as he was familiar with the layout of the house, wandered around at will. When it came to mealtime, I placed his food on the plate and told him where each item was located using clock directions: meat at 6:00, potatoes at 9:00, etc. We followed the same routine when we went to a restaurant, and it worked well as I always sat next to him to help him eat.

At night, when we shared a bed once again, I told Paul to wake me up if he needed me. But with his walker next to him, he navigated on his own when necessary. A small lamp lit the bedroom and I kept a night light on in the bathroom, the light reflecting off a mirror, so he could find his way. But he had to remember to make a left or right turn to reach the bathroom. Sometimes I would wake up to the sound of his walker hitting a wall because he became lost. He was intent on his independence and didn't want to disturb me.

Paul had developed a habit, when the night aides were taking care of him, to eat his peanut butter and jelly snack in the middle of the night. Therefore, I left a night light on in the kitchen to fulfill that desire. I made sure that the peanut butter, jelly, and crackers were always in the same spot on the shelf if he wished to retrieve them, which he did often. He managed very well, with a few exceptions. Sometimes he got lost after making a wrong turn. But he was intent on taking care of himself and I did what I could to help.

I made sure that Paul kept involved with social settings. We went to clubs for entertainment; music to listen to; storyteller clubs to participate in; discussion groups to relate with, and shows to witness. The shows were musicals that he was familiar with, and he could hum or quietly sing along to some of the tunes. When you lose your sight, life is still open for you. There is no need to vegetate. We're aware that even with the loss of a limb, individuals learn to adapt.

One time when we signed up for golf, a gentleman was added to our round. He only had the use of one arm, but he was so adept at hitting that golf ball that he outplayed us.

Another time, we were in a bowling league and played with a gentleman who had a physical impairment: one arm that only had a small extension from the shoulder, so that it was half an arm. Watching him bowl was quite a revelation.

When I was driving him, I would tell Paul that someday, with new technology, he would drive a car again. "Just tell it where you want to go. The future is amazing in this new technological world." It is starting to happen now.

Paul learned a lot about the changes he had to make in his life, once again with the assistance of the VA. They arranged a class for him in Birmingham, Alabama. He boarded a flight from Tampa on a nonstop flight, the same as an "unaccompanied minor," the flight attendant watching over his needs. Basically, he was an "unaccompanied senior."

In Birmingham, he was met at the gate, and taken to his accommodation. He dressed himself with the help of a device that when placed next to a garment, announced what color it was. He was given one of these to bring home, but it never worked well. He was expected to make his own bed and do his own laundry. He lost a few socks, but we know that washing machines do have the habit of eating socks. He was taught many skills. Though his stay was supposed to be for four weeks, after only a few, he had an episode with his back that put him in the hospital. I had to go to Birmingham to bring him home.

Adapting is the key to everything life throws at you, and we all need to realize that. For my husband, his last year and a half of life was fulfilling because he learned to accept the changes and that let him love me again. I held on to my dream and my Prince Charming lifted me up and brought me the joy of my life as we faced whatever we had to overcome together.

SNAPSHOT 38

MY PARENTS STORY

Who are we without our parents? They inspired us into becoming who we are.

My parents appeared to get along with each other very well when I was a young child. Later, I learned the truth.

My parents: Rose and Arthur

My parents married when Mom was eighteen and my father twenty-one. It was not unusual to marry that young in 1928. Mom was born in America in 1911, in what became a family of six children. Being next to the oldest child, her education ended in grade school, and she never continued on to high school, because it was necessary for her to go to work. However, she was still able to prove herself as a bookkeeper.

My mother was a quiet and kind person, dedicated to her family. She made sure my brother and I were taken care of. My Dad, on the other hand, was outgoing in personality and worked long hours as a ladies handbag leather cutter. He was the disciplinarian when necessary. I don't remember having long conversations with them, and sadly, never asked about their lives growing up. Neither did my brother, so we missed out on an opportunity to know what our parents' lives were like as they grew up and into adulthood. I knew that my father was born in 1907 and that he came from Poland, an area where the border changed and became Austria. His mother and her four children traveled from the Netherlands on a ship called the Rotterdam, and reached the United States, where her husband and older son waited for them. The Rotterdam was the first in a long line of Rotterdams belonging to the Holland America cruise line. I never asked how my father's mom handled herself and her children to get to the Netherlands from Austria. It must have been a daunting experience. Wouldn't that have been interesting to know?

When I was around nine or ten years of age, I became aware that my Mom had emotional problems. Sometimes, when I came home from school, I discovered that she had fainted or was distraught. The neighbors were taking care of her until she could handle herself to get up to her apartment on the fourth floor. Other times, she went away to a "milk farm," which was a rehab for women. She would be gone for a week or two. My brother was five years older than me, and he would take care of me during those times while my father was at work.

Now that I think about it, the next three apartments that my parents chose were always on the fourth floor. Again, I never asked what significance that meant to them.

You might think me not asking about my parents' lives as a youth was strange, but after we retired and lived in The Villages, we became part of a discussion group, and the topic came up about how our parents' lives influenced us. The conversation went around the room with about twelve people, and everyone said the same thing, "I never asked." I have also spoken to others around my age, and the answers were always the same, "I never asked." What was wrong with our generation? Did we just accept our parents without wondering about how they went through life? Did we lack curiosity? Inquisitiveness? How shallow we were as individuals not to want to know more about our history.

Just before I married, Mom and Dad went into their own business together,

making ladies handbags, which were fashioned for the businesswoman who went to work with her hat and gloves. The bags were small, compact in size. The business flourished with Mom as the bookkeeper who ran the front office and both of them designing the handbags. My father was the leather cutter, who supervised his crew who assembled, and mass produced, the handbags on their sewing machines. Sometimes, my Mom would say that she had more common sense than some of the people she came in contact with, who they relied on for their livelihood. My parents were together 24/7, and the stress of the business began to take a toll on my mother. Eventually, she wanted my father to give up the business, which he declined to do. Emotions came into play and Mom took an overdose of pills in an attempt to end her life.

SNAPSHOT 39

TAKING CARE OF MOM

D ad discovered the suicide attempt in the middle of the night. He found the pill bottle open and some pills in the sink. He did not call me until later the next morning. He wanted Paul to come to his house and bring Mom to our apartment. What a shock when I saw them practically dragging her along the hallway of our apartment house. Mom was pretty much out of it. I had started the coffee pot and made sure that she drank many cups.

I found it bewildering that my father never contacted a doctor or a hospital when he made the discovery, so that she could get help. To me, that would have been the normal response. He said, "I watched her to make sure she was breathing." That sounded foolish to Paul and to me. We realized that we were in charge of Mom now because my father went off to open his business. That was a surprise to us. He could have called and asked someone else to take charge, but he went and left us to help Mom.

My brother was living in Chicago, and it was now my responsibility to take care of my mother. She slept with my daughter, Debra, who was around five or six years of age, while

Judy was still in her crib. We sought medical advice. The doctors diagnosed Mom and recommended that she undergo shock treatment. Getting a friend to watch my children, I took Mom for her treatment. It was the worst situation I was ever involved in. I had to sit in the room while they administered the shock device and stay with her until she revived. It was like being in a torture chamber, watching a monster take control of my mother. I felt like I was in an out-of-body world and my Mom was an alien, not the kind and gentle person who had taken care of me. It was a nightmare.

I do not remember how many treatments Mom had. The doctor did not suggest any other therapy to help her deal with her situation. My father was not involved in this at all. When he came to my house for dinner while Mom lived with me, he was actually a hindrance. He always said the wrong things to her. She would be calm, and at peace, when my Dad would ask her about something he thought she should remember. When she did not acknowledge remembering, he could not fathom why she could not recall what he did. I could see Mom tense right up. The treatments had affected her memory. I tried to make my father understand, but he just continued on his path of annoying her with his prodding.

Over time, I began to dislike my father. No matter how I explained the situation to him, it fell on deaf ears. It was as though he had not heard a word I said. It was like talking to a wall.

My father later arranged for a cottage by the beach, hoping it would rejuvenate Mom, which it appeared to do.

After the stay at the beach, their lives seemed to go back to normal, but Mom never went back to work with my Dad. They had their friends and would get together with them again. The men played cards and the ladies played mahjongg, which was a Chinese game that became popular with Americans. My father always seemed to be a devoted husband and often remarked that they were a great and loving couple. All appeared to be going well.

SNAPSHOT 40

BEHIND CLOSED DOORS

Many years later, with Dad retired, my parents moved to a retirement community in Florida. They found enjoyment with new friends and some old friends who followed them there. Visiting them when we moved to Tampa, I began to detect a slight odor emanating from Mom's pores and realized she was upset. She would never enlighten me when I asked if something was bothering her. I began to suspect that they really didn't have the good relationship that we were led to believe they had. As the saying goes, "You never know what goes on behind closed doors."

At the age of sixty-four, Mom had already developed angina. As it worsened, her cardiologist suggested a new procedure called a bypass, that would take care of the angina, and last for at least five years. As it turned out, it lasted ten years, and when her condition worsened, a second bypass was suggested. However, it was dangerous because of her age, which was now seventy-four. The angina was a major problem. The doctors said she could have a stroke if she did not have the surgery. Mom had to make a difficult decision. She didn't want to be dependent or a burden on anyone, so she chose to have the surgery.

I went to see her in the hospital prior to the operation. We hugged and cried together. The realization overtook me that this might be the last time I would see or speak to my mother. I was saying goodbye. The person that gave me life, that I loved my whole life, might be giving up her life. It was as if a part of me was about to be removed, and the surgeon's knife was separating us forever.

Unfortunately, she did not survive the operation.

Mom's funeral was just prior to the Jewish holiday of Yom Kippur. As was the custom, we could not "sit shiva," our period of mourning. Normally after the funeral, friends and family come to express their caring and understanding that we were hurting. It felt strange when people did not come to pay their respects at Dad's home. This was painful and left us no closure.

Paul and I stayed about a week to help my father, and then we went home to Tampa. When I saw my Rabbi after we returned, at Shabbat services, the only thing he said was, "How are you doing, Sandy?" and then he walked away. He did not even stop to talk, to help me get over my sadness. I was hurt that this was the extent of his caring. A year or more later, after the temple faced a difficult situation, I was glad when they hired a new Rabbi.

A few years after, Paul's father died, and the Rabbi came to our home to be with Paul. I mentioned losing my Mom and how badly the previous Rabbi handled my grief. Our new Rabbi told me he would meet privately with me, and we would work together through my grief. That is what a clergyman is supposed to do. It was good to talk through the loss of my mother with a Rabbi who showed his compassion.

What I found most interesting after Mom passed, was that

my father became a different person. It was as though he was released from responsibility and moved into another dimension. It felt like a new dawn, an awakening that I had not felt in him for a long time. Could I actually love this man again? I loved Mom dearly, and as my mother's name was Rose, I sent her a dozen roses every Mother's Day. Could I ever feel this kind of love for my father?

SNAPSHOT 41

REDISCOVERING DAD

I had given up on my father when I could not tolerate how he treated my mother. I was not sure I could ever love him again, but after Mom died, I saw him change. His humorous side, and his willingness to take on a new life, surprised me. I am not saying that he did not love my Mom through fifty-six years of marriage, but it was apparent that he could not handle her depressions.

Dad found a group of widows and widowers, who got together to enjoy the rest of their lives. I met the group on different occasions, and they were a fun bunch who supported each other. For the next ten years, my Dad enjoyed their times together, and I felt like I began to know a different father. I did not want to lose my mom, but rediscovered my dad, because of her passing. It was a strange feeling for a daughter.

Over the years, Dad went through colon cancer and his eyesight got worse. He had sight problems when Mom was alive. He would say that she was his navigator when he drove the car. We were concerned with his ability to continue driving, but he would remark, "It's okay. I know the neighborhood." He had an accident which totaled the car. Luckily, he was all right. When the insurance company offered him a loaner, he responded, "No thanks, I think God was telling me to stop driving." He negotiated with the insurance company and got $9,200 for a car that we estimated was only worth around $6,200 to $7,000. My cousin, Murray, who lived nearby, thought he should go into business with his uncle negotiating for people.

After 10 years as a widower, Dad told me that he was leaving his front door open. When I inquired why, he responded, "So they can find my body." He also told me he had a prescription for Valium and his doctor told him to take it whenever he did not feel good. "What!" I found the prescription and called his doctor who tried not to admit he gave it to my father. But it was evident the doctor did not want to be bothered.

"Okay, Dad, it's time to move to Tampa," I said, wanting to help him.

"No way," he said. "I don't want to leave my friends."

My brother, sister-in-law, Paul, and I made a 90th birthday party for our father. As we planned it, we took my dad along. He remarked, "You know, I may not make it." I replied, "It won't be a party without you." It turned out to be a delightful evening with friends and family.

I was still intent on relocating my father so he could get more help. There was an assisted living facility attached to a community center that we thought would be perfect for him. I said, "Dad, why not try it for a month? We'll rent furniture, and if you still don't like it, we'll drive you back."

As it turned out, my friend Stan's father, Charlie, was already living there. I introduced my father to Charlie by saying, "This is my father, Arthur."

It was unbelievable. Charlie was the older brother of Dad's

best friend, Murray. Dad often hung out at their house in New York. Murray had already died. What a revelation! Dad and Charlie had not seen each other for seventy years. My father stayed at the assisted living facility, and they became best friends for the next two-and-a-half years, when my dad passed on.

My father would often tell us that we didn't have to worry about his burial. It was all paid for. "Just know I have one request. I want a bottle of Dewar's Scotch to go with me in the coffin."

Paul answered, "Can I drink some of it first?"

We made sure at the funeral that a bottle of Dewar's went into the coffin.

I miss both my parents and dwell on the good memories to overcome the sad ones. No relationship is perfect, so I try to think of the good times and not the bad.

SNAPSHOT 42

A GROWING FAMILY

Grandchildren become the joy of your life. I've heard quotes like, "You take all the pleasure of being with grandkids, but then give them back to their parents, and it's stress free." In other words, you can enjoy the best parts and not be too stressed out by the rest. Paul and I were not able to abide by that idea. Unfortunately, we were grandparents too far away to watch our grandkids grow up. What an opportunity we missed. One family lived in New York, the other in Colorado, and we lived in Tampa, Florida. Our next-door neighbors had children the same ages as my grandchildren in New York, so we watched their children grow up parallel to our own.

The term we used at the time was "nuclear family" because so many families did not live near each other. I recall when Debra announced she was pregnant, the same evening that Paul revealed he was being transferred to Tampa. I said, "We can't leave, this is not a good time." His response was, "There will never be a good time." We were two couples conflicted by wonderful news and a sad realization at the same time.

Ronnie

Deidre

Megan

Sean

MY GRANDCHILDREN

My first grandchild was Megan, in New York. She sparkled from the beginning of life, whenever we had the chance to be with her. But we were lucky to get to see her once a year when we flew up to Clintondale for a visit.

Sean arrived two years later, and Debra and Mike came to Tampa six months after that. Expecting it to be warm in March, they had not thought to bring warm clothes with them, and we had to shop for sweaters for the children. Tampa was a surprise to us when we arrived, unaware of the fact that the weather could get cold in the winter months. "We're down south. How did that happen?"

As the years went by, and our grandchildren got older, we realized that we could spend quality time with the kids if they came to Tampa without Mommy and Daddy. We thought it would be even better if the kids came one at a time, but Sean would not come without Megan. When we were confident that the grandchildren were safe to fly, they became "unaccompanied minors." Arrangements were made in New York. The stewardess would watch over them on the flight, and Paul and I would meet them at the gate in Tampa. It worked beautifully, and we all enjoyed our time together.

We took Megan and Sean to Disney World, the beaches on both coasts, and Busch Gardens, which was in Tampa. One time in Disney World, as we were waiting in a line for refreshments, Sean saw money on the floor. He picked up a $100.00 bill. Quickly, he pocketed it, and when we all sat down, Megan was encouraging him to spend it. Not Sean. He was bringing it home to show his parents. We were amazed at his good luck. When he got home and was thinking of what he was going to buy with it, he, unfortunately, ran into a dilemma.

Being a kid, Sean was lax in taking care of his things. One day, his retainer for his teeth, which had been in braces, disappeared. When the retainer was found, it was damaged. My daughter and son-in-law were upset with him because they had to keep reminding him to be responsible for his possessions. The decision was made that the $100.00 bill would pay for a new retainer.

Another time, Megan came down to Tampa by herself. She was fifteen or sixteen years old. We took her canoeing. The fellow in charge was explaining how to handle the canoe and watch out for alligators. Megan was not paying attention to him.

We got in the canoe, Megan in front, me in the middle, and Paul in the back. As we came around a bend, Megan was staring at a baby alligator perched on a small ledge. Of course, she let out a scream which scared the rest of us. When we all calmed down, we saw we were not in any danger. Believe me, Megan was alert for the rest of the trip.

Megan loved going to the beach, but she was very fair-skinned, so we had to keep reminding her to not get burnt from the hot sun. But she wanted to go home with a tan. She laid out on a blanket with that goal in mind. Ironically, instead of a tan, her skin turned red and peeled away. She went home without the tan she wanted.

Paul and I loved the chance to be with our grandchildren and made the arrangements to do the same with our Colorado grandkids. They lived in Aurora, which is a suburb of Denver. Deidre was around eleven years old and was coming to Tampa for Thanksgiving week. Actually, Deidre has the same birthday as her Aunt Debra, March 17, so we have two St. Patrick Day's girls. The arrangements were made for Deidre to fly from Denver as an "unaccompanied minor." Because of the two-hour time difference between Denver and Tampa, the plane was scheduled to arrive around 1:00 AM in Tampa.

Her father, Ron, took Deidre to the airport, while Judy waited at home with her younger brother, Ronnie. The stewardess put Deidre on the plane and an ice storm arrived. Deidre was removed from the plane while they deiced the wings. That took a considerable amount of time. Ron contacted Judy with the news, and Judy, as nervous as can be, believed they should cancel the whole trip. Not Deidre. She still wanted to go.

After the plane was prepared, they placed Deidre back inside, but more problems arose with ice accumulating. Off the plane she goes again.

In the meantime, Paul and I, in Tampa, were getting phone calls back and forth. She's coming. No, she's not. She's coming. No, she's not. After many hours, and making sure it is safe, the plane is loaded again, and finally departs. Instead of arriving in Tampa at around 1:00 AM, Deidre arrived around 5:00 AM. We were all groggy from not getting a night's sleep. We stopped for breakfast and then headed home and right to bed.

It was a wonderful week with Deidre as we went to Disney World, and wandered around lots of places the rest of the time she was with us. Flying back home was not complicated at all. All three of us had great memories of our shared time together.

A few years later, when Ronnie was nine, he visited from Colorado. He was a trooper, raring to go. Off we went to Disney World, and Ronnie was so excited. He was going to go on every ride. In Hollywood Studios there is an attraction called "The Twilight Zone Tower Of Terror," and Ronnie knew all about it. He wanted us to go with him.

Paul never enjoyed thrill rides. Even though as a teenager I went on all the thrill rides in Coney Island, as an adult, I had become more fearful. "No," we tell Ronnie. "We're not going on that ride."

Ronnie made up his mind. This young boy was all excited and a daredevil. We made sure the ride was safe, asking an attendant. We were told, "It's okay. He'll be fine."

I waited with Ronnie as the line moved slowly along. Ronnie was talking to everyone around him. Someone told him that The Tower Of Terror is a scary elevator drop in the dark. As we got closer to the entrance, Ronnie suddenly announced, "I don't want to go. Let's go back." I was relieved because I was concerned about his safety.

We were staying at a hotel nearby and had plans to return to another Disney park the next day. During the night, I woke up with severe pain in my back. I was not sure what was going on but surmised that it was shingles. Though we were all disappointed, we needed to return to Tampa.

Because it was Sunday, we went to an urgent care facility. The doctors were uncertain of the cause but gave me medication for the pain. The next day, I went to my primary doctor, who confirmed I had shingles.

For the rest of Ronnie's stay with us, we found other fun things to do. We enjoyed our grandson's visit with us. I only wish I did not have shingles at the time.

The program of having young kids traveling as "unaccompanied minors" was well organized by the airplane industry. We sent our daughter, Judy, when she was eleven years old, to Houston, Texas, where good friends and their sons were reuniting after they moved away. As a travel agent, I had arranged other family reunions with their "unaccompanied minors." Our idea to bring our grandchildren to Tampa over the many years we lived there was a success because it gave us the opportunity to get to know each other better. We felt fulfillment as grandparents. Many families are separated from each other for many different reasons, but no one should give up the chance to make a difference in their grandchildren's lives.

Our grandchildren are adults now with their own children. Megan has an eight-year-old son, Cameron, who challenges teachers because of his intelligence. Megan worked in many different jobs, but the last one was as a phlebotomist, taking blood from people for lab tests.

Sean married Eve, a young woman from Thailand. They have two sons, Eoin and Rian. Because of his Irish roots, their last name is O'Reilly, so he chose Irish names for his kids. He's a barber with his own shop.

Deidre, with her husband, Matt, has two children, Maxton, and Mae. She is a financial advisor in her own business.

Ronnie is in the Navy, stationed in Guantanamo, Cuba, with his wife, Sara. They have two children, Georgia and Teddy.

All my grandchildren and great-grandchildren now live in Florida, except for Ronnie's family. He is in the Navy, which he says he wants to make his career.

I'm proud to be a great-grandmother of seven, whom they call GG, and watch my family grow. I do not want to miss the opportunity to watch them grow up.

SNAPSHOT 43

WHERE IN THE WORLD ARE SANDY AND PAUL?

Frolicking on cruise destinations

Our lives were always changing. With our children married, Paul and I were now independent and looking for different horizons. I always wanted to see the world and now was the right time. Wherever we went, we found various locations and cultures exciting. They were diverse and poles apart from our lives in the United States.

In celebration of our 25th anniversary, we were leaving the United States for the first time on a trip to Israel. We were living in Poughkeepsie at the time. I was not yet a travel agent. It was 1979, and I was very excited and yet nervous. I felt like how Columbus must have felt when he set out across an ocean towards a new land, uncertain what he was about to discover.

It was a very long flight on El Al Airlines, about eleven hours. We arrived having not slept overnight. As we greet the other members of the tour, we learned that we came from all parts of the United States, so we had a lot to learn together.

As we toured Israel, we discovered that the Israelis transformed a biblical wasteland into modern cities and communities, and yet preserved the archeological sites that are throughout the country. We were amazed as we visited these sites, going back centuries in time. It was like taking a very stimulating history lesson. Sixty percent of Israel's land was desert. Since 1948, they have planted more than two hundred sixty-five million trees. The trees help provide water for its citizens and for farming. The trees draw moisture from the atmosphere and, with drip irrigation and placing pipes, water is channeled throughout the land.

We visited Jerusalem, one of the holiest cities in the world. We were surprised to learn all the stone in Jerusalem comes from the same quarry. Every building, new or old, uses the same stone, so you are looking at a city of the same color, a mix of tan and rust. After hearing so much about this holy city, and what it means to Jews, we are here, about to enter it. Sitting on the bus, we heard familiar music. It was Jerusalem of Gold. I could not control the tears flowing from my eyes.

Walking through the ancient streets connected us to the multiple generations that led their lives here. It was always the crossroads of civilization and the heart of our faith.

After Jerusalem, we went to the Dead Sea. You can only float in the Dead Sea and not sink because of the high salt content and the sulphur, which smelled like rotten eggs. I could not believe we were here but unhappy it smelled so bad. Everybody said it was healthy, but even a shower did not wash away the awful smell.

We vowed to return to this exciting country as new technology continues to make it the foremost destination for tourism. However, soon after our return, I became a travel agent, and my focus was on exploring the rest of the world.

Where in the world are Sandy and Paul?

We became world travelers and what an adventure that was. Along the way, I was a winner in many respects. Participating in a travel agent contest, I won one thousand dollars.

Before leaving Poughkeepsie in 1981, we flew to Hawaii, where we visited all four islands. Each had different topography, history, and artifacts. On the Big Island, in the area of Hilo, lush settings and huge green plants were quite a sight because they get approximately two hundred inches of rain a year.

We stayed at a hotel right next to the most active volcano, Kilauea. It started erupting again months later, adding landmass to the island with its lava flows.

At the Polynesian Cultural Center in Oahu, they put on a show, as we sat in small boats that traverse the center through canals. At each stop, a guide details the culture of each island in the Pacific near Hawaii. It was a wonderful visit to our beautiful state.

In 1984, we were off to Spain. From Don Quixote to castles and walled cities, we enjoyed it all. Flamenco dancers were a treat to watch while we feasted on their food specialties. We purchased famous Lladro sculptures. We learned that there was a special area on the plane to secure the Lladro.

Spain's culture was also interesting. Because of their midday siesta, dinner is usually around 10:00 PM, so we became night owls.

Back to the South Pacific in 1986. The flight took twenty-one hours. We tried to focus on the places we were visiting: Tahiti, New Zealand, and Australia. New Zealand was our favorite because of the beauty of its green fields all around you. There are more sheep than people; 18 varieties producing wool for New Zealand's primary industry.

In Australia, we spent New Year's Eve at the famous opera house in Sydney. Walking through the zoo allowed us to meet some unusual animals up close and personal. A kangaroo ate right out of my hand and a koala loved to be petted. We snorkeled in the Great Barrier Reef, the longest reef in the world. There, we saw unusual fish in the most colorful and magnificent coral settings.

1987 brought us to Mexico. We watched cliff divers in Acapulco and enjoyed our beach resort set in a semicircle. Paul climbed a pyramid in Mexico City, which was quite a feat, definitely not for anyone with a fear of height. Getting down was more of a problem, but the structures were amazing to see.

We went to a Mexican Fiesta where I was part of the fashion show. What fun! Mariachi music rounded out all the festivities.

We discovered the Orient was our favorite destination because the culture is so different from ours. We traveled mostly on our own, hiring private guides to take us sightseeing. We set out in 1986 to Hong Kong, which is a mixture of different worlds, Asian and Western. We enjoyed it before Britain gave it back to China. There are multiple skyscrapers on this tiny island.

On to Singapore, which is modern, clean, and the safest place to wander on your own. We took a "Contrasting Cultures" tour, which focused on the mix of Indian, Malay, and Chinese cultures. They are all different from each other yet blending well.

In Thailand, there was the most beautiful architecture and sculptures we ever saw. They were made of precious stones, jade, and mother of pearl. Absolutely stunning. Unique were their floating markets, selling their goods from boat to boat. We were there in March, and it was the hottest climate we ever experienced. It was like stepping into an oven.

Japan was our next stop, where friends were representing IBM on a three-year assignment. They became our tour guides. The cherry blossoms were in bloom. They are native to Japan and were a gorgeous background to all the incredible sites.

We became familiar with Buddhas and kabuki performances. The ancient architecture was unique when compared to their modern cities. We learned to navigate their rail systems and order at restaurants with the help of our friends.

An uncomfortable feature in some of the Asian countries like Thailand and Japan, as well as China, which we visited years later, was their toilets. They do not have commodes, but instead use a hole in the ground. I imagined the women in earlier years in Japan, wearing kimonos and trying to keep the garment away from your body while using these facilities. I had enough difficulty in western garb.

At the airport in Tokyo, they had Western and Eastern toilets. Asians believe that their methods are more sanitary because the body doesn't touch the toilet.

In 1989, we had Italy as the destination in our sights. We went from one city to the next, and took in all the famous sites: the Vatican; Coliseum; Trevi Fountain; Leaning Tower of Pisa; the massive statue of Michelangelo's David, and embarked on a gondola ride on the unique waterways of Venice.

Back in Asia, in 1992, we journeyed to Malaysia. I won the trip at a travel agent seminar. The architecture was beautiful, and the markets impressed us with different varieties of fruits and vegetables that we never saw or tasted before.

We went to a snake temple that held a large number of venomous snakes. As we walked around, the snakes were not aggressive due to a form of incense in the air that drugged them.

Top spinning is a cultural activity, and we watched the competitions. The tops are wound up so tightly that they can spin for about an hour, with a little oil added for lubrication.

At our hotel, we noticed an arrow on the ceiling and inquired about its significance. We were told the arrow pointed to Mecca, the holiest site for this Muslim nation.

Another highlight of our travels was Great Britain in 1993. We rented an apartment in London with friends and wandered about as if we were English natives. We had to get used to the traffic coming from a different direction. We used their buses and underground to maneuver around the royal residences and beyond. We even went to Dover, where we stood on the beach singing "The White Cliffs of Dover," the famous song from World War II. And yes, the cliffs were white.

We spent a week on a bus trip throughout England. We toured Stratford on Avon, York and the southern part of Scotland in Edinburgh, where I ate haggis. Not bad. Stonehenge was also part of the mix.

Crossing back across the ocean, we visited the Canadian Rockies in 1995, with its different topography of majestic mountains and lush scenery. Moose roamed like they belonged there, which they did. It was their land. Most impressive was Victoria with its huge Butchart Gardens. It was the most beautiful all-around garden retreat that I ever saw, with a mix of plants and colors that were spectacular on acres and acres of land.

Totem poles were the norm in Ketchikan, Alaska, as we cruised the Inside Passage in 1996 and witnessed the glaciers. They were massive, in shades of blue. But it was cold, and I huddled beneath the blanket for warmth. And this was in July!

From Anchorage, we traveled by rail up to Fairbanks, which is more or less a western-style town near the Arctic Circle. It was interesting to note that it was daylight there for almost twenty-four hours. It did not affect our sleeping habits with special shades on the windows.

In 1997, with friends, we traveled to the Atlantic Maritimes in Eastern Canada.

Between Nova Scotia and New Brunswick, there were reversing falls. We stood on a bridge and watched the water reverse. Boats waited until the right moment before they could continue moving. At the Bay of Fundy, in New Brunswick, we could walk on the ocean floor when the tide was out. But you had to get out of the seafloor before the tide came back in. There was a clock to notify you when to leave. If you didn't make it, there was a staircase where you could wait until the tide went out again, about six hours later.

Lobster was plentiful, and we enjoyed the delicious crustaceans. Just thinking about them makes my mouth water.

A year later, in 1998, we took a cruise from Singapore to Australia. Bali, Indonesia was the highlight when I think of a magical place. The architecture was dazzling and there were beautiful temples everywhere. Each family has a shrine of various sizes in their backyard.

Lush, tropical rice terraces and statues draped in cloth are everywhere you go. The colors have religious meaning.

In 2000, the turn of the century, China was on our calendar. It is a world of centuries past. As we went from location to location, we felt as if we had stepped back in history.

In Xian, we saw the famous Terra Cotta warriors, built 2,000 years ago. We were surprised that most had been broken by an invading army centuries ago. The sculptures were unearthed in the 1970s and are being restored. There were eight thousand warriors in amazing detail, each face with different features. There are also horses and chariots to complement the army. All were constructed to protect the first emperor after he died and entered the next world.

The Great Wall of China definitely belongs as one of the Seven Wonders of the World. It is amazing that thousands of years ago, they built this wall over mountains for a distance of three thousand miles. It boggles your mind as to how they did it. For me, it was an endurance test to climb this very steep area for about a quarter-mile up the mountain, walking on the irregular steps. It was even more difficult trying to come back down. The steps are so steep that you had to hold yourself at a backward slant, and at some points, I had to just sit down and let my butt take me down.

We enjoyed being a part of an old world where they are adjusting to a new world. The fashions and vehicles are much like western norms.

Our last international adventure was in Scandinavia in the latter part of 2000. We visited old western civilizations like Sweden, Denmark, and Norway. There were palaces and colorful buildings throughout, most notably the fjords of Norway, where the mountains meet the sea. Viking ships were on display, reminding us of their missions and desire to seek out other lands, as Sandy and Paul chose to do.

From 1980 to 2013, we cannot forget our beautiful United States. We've traveled and experienced the wonders of 47 states through Elderhostel educational programs, as well as independently. Our country has highlights that other countries cannot match. One example is our amazing National Park System. We were amazed at how different they are from each other. They are spectacular in their natural state. My favorite was Bryce Canyon, with its colorful rock formations in orange, yellow, and red. It looked as if it was painted.

Cruising has also been one of our great pleasures. Ships have taken us to all the Caribbean islands, the coasts of Mexico and Central America, and the Mediterranean.

Crazy fun on a cruise with friends

All told, our feet have walked incredibly in forty-eight countries. It has been an amazing journey and opportunity to experience different cultures. We met people whose lives and traditions make them all the more colorful. A wonderful part of what Paul and I learned is the mosaic of civilization.

When you spend a lifetime together, there is so much that you've shared. Both Paul's life and mine have been enhanced beyond our imagination by all the wonderful places we visited.

SNAPSHOT 44

GOLF AND LIFE

The game of golf is friendly, fun, and frustrating. Somewhere in the middle of all this is skill.

Playing since the early 70s, I never was a good golfer but enjoyed getting out on the course. Because I ended up walking a lot, I thought it was also good exercise. I did get a hole-in-one but do not consider that to be because of skill. I teed off on a short hole and it landed in the cup. Pure luck. But I certainly enjoyed the moment.

My husband and I enjoyed playing golf together, and in the locales where we lived, we did not need to have others pair up with us. In New Jersey, we were playing an eighteen-hole course that was quite hilly. My daughter, Judy, at twelve years old, was my caddy. Walking throughout, swinging and swinging, I got very tired. At one point, my ball landed on top of a hill near the hole. I climbed the hill, putted the ball in, laid down, and rolled down the hill.

Paul told me that other golfers stopped playing, looked stunned, and then burst into laughter. You definitely have to have a sense of humor for this game.

Paul and I were playing a round, and at one juncture was a

grove of trees. Paul teed off. Instead of the ball going straight ahead, the ball hits a tree to his right. He gets another ball, tees off, and the ball hits the same tree. He says, after trying again with another two balls, "If I hit that damn tree again, I'm throwing the second ball down the fairway."

He gets set, hits the ball, and, unbelievably, hits the same tree. So, he throws the other ball down the fairway. Now, even a pro cannot do that. I just started laughing and laughing.

My friend Sunny lives in Arizona, in a Del Webb senior community. She was playing golf and her ball landed on someone's lawn. She went to retrieve it and the property owner would not let her get the ball. He told her to get off his lawn. She said, "You're kidding. Why did you buy a house adjacent to a golf course?"

The owner remained firm, so Sunny went back to her golf cart and got another ball. She walked back to the man and handed him the ball. "What's this for?" the man asked.

Sunny's response was, "Every prick needs two balls."

In contrast, here in The Villages, at one course where I was playing, I teed off my ball and it landed on someone's lawn. I went to retrieve it and saw a white ball in the grass. I could not lift it because it was glued to the ground. I moved to another spot thinking there was my ball. That one was also glued down. That homeowner had a sense of humor.

When we moved to Tampa in 1982, our home was directly across from a golf course. We thought that we would be playing a lot of golf, so I decided to go to the pro for advice. He asked, "What's your problem?"

I responded, "I can't count that high."

His retort was, "Are you in a tournament?"

"No."

"Then why are you counting?"

Paul and I both stopped counting, and would just play for the enjoyment. Here I am, almost 20 years later in The Villages, and I'm still not counting.

SNAPSHOT 45

JUNE 2017: PRINCE CHARMING

In June 2017, Paul's medical problems resurfaced. He was sent back and forth to hospitals and rehab. It ended with Paul being sent to Hospice where he died on September 6, 2017.

Before he died, I was thankful most of our family was able to see Paul because it was Labor Day. Unfortunately, our grandson, Ronnie, who was in the Navy, stationed in Japan, could not be with us but called to talk to his Grandpa.

The next day, our temple choir leader, Michele, came to sing to him. She brought other choir members with her. Even as Paul lapsed into a coma, the doctor said he could still hear the music. Hearing is the last sense to go.

The following day, Paul was still in a coma. I was told that his life would end shortly. I climbed into bed with him and reminded him of the wonderful years we had together, the love that would never depart from my heart. I told him I would be all right, and it was okay for him to go.

Shortly after, the doctor reentered the room. He took Paul's pulse and said Paul was gone. I felt I gave my husband permission to leave.

Now that the time had come, and my sweet love was no longer with me, the numbness settled in. The light in my life was gone and darkness took over. I realized it was inevitable in life that we pass on, but you always wish it would come much later.

I am crying as I write this, which I have not done for a long time. I am surprised that emotions still come to the surface even after three and a half years since I lost him.

There is a plaque on the memorial wall at our temple that states, PAUL SOLOMON, A WONDERFUL LIFE. It is something he would always tell me. It states the same on the wall at Bushnell National Military Cemetery where he is interred.

What sustains me is I tell myself how lucky we were. How many people can say they were married 63 years? I feel as if I won the lottery, which I did, by meeting Paul.

Initially, I spoke to Paul every day after he passed. I would say jokingly, "He doesn't answer. But sometimes he didn't answer when he was alive."

As the years pass, I only communicate with Paul sometimes now, when there's a memory that comes to mind. But every day, I think of him because he was my life.

SNAPSHOT 46

THE JOY OF FAMILY

My daughters Judy and Debra: My Closest Connection

Our daughters are all grown up now. Each has a caring husband and a good marriage. They have their own families, each with a daughter and a son. Incredibly, my little girls are now grandmothers, which makes me a great-grandmother, called GG. I love that.

In years past, we were all separated, living in states far apart. Judy was in Colorado, Debra in New York, and Paul and I were in Florida. It was not easy to get together and see each other. After many years apart, we were pleasantly surprised that our daughters and their husbands chose to move to Florida. Each of them is now within a one-and-a-quarter-hour drive from our home, but far from each other. As we are in the middle, many times, they will meet at our home for different occasions. I'd say we were very lucky, compared to our friends whose children live far away from them. Having them close to me now has been a blessing.

Debra continues to work as a nurse, and Judy works as a manager at a finance company. I am proud of both of them and my grandchildren. Ironically, Debra's husband, Mike, worked for IBM and then started his own business. When they moved to Florida, he worked for the state Department of Transportation. Judy's husband, Ron, also worked for IBM and then for AT&T. Both of my sons-in-law and Debra are now retired. I guess we're all getting old.

My two daughters mean the most to me at this time in my life. Now that I am widowed, they are a great support system. They each helped me deal with Paul's death and the complexities of continuing to live my life. I have a daughter who is a nurse to soothe me, and a daughter who is a financial adviser to help me handle my finances. I love them both.

A Trio of Love

I have once again found pleasure in life. I wake each day with a purpose, to fulfill each minute the most I can. That is what Paul would have wanted.

Epilogue

I mentioned at the beginning of this collection of snapshots that Paul and I taught English to a Russian immigrant couple while we lived in Poughkeepsie in the 70s. Their names were Boris and Irena. As they became more and more fluent and comfortable with English, they told us that, in Russia, bad news is never reported.

In the town where they lived, one day there suddenly was a rumbling sound. Boris was outside the house and yelled to Irena to get their daughter and run from their home.

Irena got her daughter out before the earthquake hit, but she stayed, standing in front of her breakfront, holding it up so all the dishes would not break. Thankfully, the earthquake was not that intense in magnitude, and all turned out well.

Paul and I were on a Mediterranean cruise many years later and were sitting at a table with six strangers. They were discussing weather phenomena, and I was relating the story of Irena and Boris' earthquake.

A man suddenly remarked, "I know that story."

"Huh?"

The man said, "I am on this cruise with Boris and Irena's cousins," and he brings us to them. They had heard about Paul and me as Boris and Irena's English instructors and we all had a nice conversation. It shows again what a small world it really is. You never know how someone you meet can impact your life or the lives of others.

Life, according to the dictionary, is the sum of experiences and actions that constitute a person's existence. I see it as the ability to adapt to your environment and bring meaning to each event and person you encounter.

In this book, I touched on a life filled to the brim with experiences and memories that made me the woman I am today. I feel I achieved my life goals and, if anything, surpassed my expectations. I wake up each day with the knowledge that I have traveled down my own path to fulfillment and tasted the fruits of understanding so much along the way.

When I think back on my life, I realize that I have been more than lucky. I was blessed with being married to a wonderful man and will always miss Paul. We raised two caring and loving daughters, who gave us beautiful grandkids we adore and who have accomplished so much. We had a life full of travel and the joy of learning about different lands and cultures. Along our path, we met and enjoyed wonderful friends.

Yes, there were obstacles and some sad times. When they came my way, I latched on and rode with them. I refused to give up on my dreams. It has been a wonderful life, and writing these snapshots reminds me of how blessed I have been. It is the blessings we must always keep in our scrapbook. Those are the snapshots of my life I have shared with you. Thank you for joining me on this journey. I hope you have a life full of wonderful snapshots too.